The

Southern Way

The regular volume for the Southern devotee

Kevin Robertson

Issue 45

www.crecy.co.uk

ISBN 9781909328860

First published in 2019 by Noodle Books
an imprint of Crécy Publishing Ltd

New contact details
All editorial submissions to:
The Southern Way (Kevin Robertson)
'Silmaril'
Upper Lambourn
Hungerford
Berkshire RG17 8QR
Tel: 01488 674143
editorial@thesouthernway.co.uk

A CIP record for this book is available from the British Library

Publisher's note: Every effort has been made to identify and correctly attribute photographic credits. Any error that may have occurred is entirely unintentional.

Printed in England by LatimerTrend

Noodle Books is an imprint of
Crécy Publishing Limited
1a Ringway Trading Estate
Shadowmoss Road
Manchester M22 5LH

www.crecy.co.uk

Front cover:
Former SECR, then East Kent Railway and finally BR 'O1' Class 0-6-0 No 31258 reverses at Shepherds Well on the occasion of the Railway Enthusiasts Club (Farnborough) tour of Saturday 23 May 1959. This trip was based around the East Kent Light Railway and its associated collieries and commenced from Shepherds Well taking the route Tilmanstone-Shepherds Well-Kearnsey-Deal-Betteshanger box-Betteshanger Colliery-Minster-Richborough Sidings-Richborough box-Deal-Kearnsey. Several reversals were necessary en route. The same engine was used throughout and, at Minster at least, was spotted carrying the headcode 'SPL77'. Two coaches and a four-wheel brake van made up the formation.
Trevor Owen courtesy of Hugh Davies

Rear cover:
Here is a genuine attempt (at least on the cover of this issue) to redress the imbalance of limited SE section material having appearing in 'SW'. Former SECR 'H' Class 0-4-4T No 31544 is seen at Eastleigh in March 1964, having drawn its last breath and now sitting to await its inevitable fate. Built in 1904, No 31544 was last allocated to Three Bridges, from where it was withdrawn at the end of 1963. It was moved to Eastleigh at the end of December and was still intact – except for the removal of the inspection plate – when seen three months later. Fitted for air-control pull-push operation, the additional Westinghouse pump is alongside the smokebox, while the coupling rods have been left in the coal space.

Title page:
The pick-up goods is something we have lost completely in recent years, and of course with it so many of the lines that such workings once served. A typical service is seen at Rudgwick on the lamented route from Guildford to Horsham in 1951 behind an unidentified 'C2x' with what also appears to be mainly empty wagons.
Edward Griffiths

Contents

Introduction

Not quite sure why', but I am starting to write this particular piece literally the day before SW43 (July) is due. I know I have a habit of trying to be early, but this time there is a genuine reason and that is a potential house move in the autumn. (If there is a new contact address it is obvious that it all worked. If not – well, these things happen.)

But to railways. A few days ago I made my first trip on what was a new bit of Southern Railway to me, the section from Guildford to Redhill. Fine, so I am possibly one of the few readers of 'SW' who have never traversed this route before and, even if today things are not perhaps the same as in the era I personally find appealing, there is still much to see. It was also only a one-way journey, so immediately questions arose: which side to sit, where and when to look out, etc, etc. Of course upon my return it was immediately out with the maps and a look at 'SW' issues 7, 12, 20 and 25 for some more historic information. (No, I do not have such a memory that I can recall exactly what went into each issue, although I can usually (?) remember if we have had a piece on a particular topic, even if it is rare that I can remember the actual issue. So thanks to Alan Postlethwaite and Mick Fields for their respective index of contents.)

On the journey 'between stations', so to speak, I was also musing on the potential contents I might include in this issue. Obvious are the pieces that had of necessity been carried over, after which comes an attempt at complying with promises made. Next a possible topic that I have seen discussed or mentioned on the net or wherever, and finally whatever happens to have been suggested or, dare I say, I have a specific interest in at the time. In the latter category there will often be topics that are impossible now to cover either in word or photographic form. So many men from the 'old days' are no longer with us, while failing health can also take its toll. As an example, I will mention one man I was told of who had been a signalman – at Fordingbridge, I think it was mentioned, an SR line that closed in the early 1960s. I was advised that in his younger days he had been a born raconteur, but sadly now refuses to see anyone and, despite attempts on my behalf, I must respect his privacy.

But all is not lost on the reminiscences front, and we are delighted to include a brief few words on shunters' duties, something we have certainly not covered before. Speaking to the individual concerned (see page <??>), the one thing I recall more than anything was when he was sent on the relief to Eastleigh for a few days. 'That was hard work, I was at it all day ... it was a relief to get away and back to Winchester,' he recounts, and I think that is the exact point of the matter, that many railwaymen worked long hours involving heavy and dirty work. Not just footplate crews either, but also the multitude of artisans behind the scenes, all absolutely necessary to keep the railway system operational. All this was accomplished with the minimum of mechanical assistance – small wonder there were very few portly loco crews, shunters or permanent way men, to give just a few examples (unlike the 'relaxed muscle' currently carried by your writer – 'she who must be obeyed' looks after me too well).

Elsewhere in this piece I am delighted to confirm the appearance of the first part of our promised article on the rationalisation of the Salisbury to Exeter line, to be followed we hope in consecutive issues with the actual singling, signalling, and revised train workings that resulted. I recall some years ago bemoaning to a friend the fact that west of Salisbury the route had been singled, but he rightly pulled me up short, saying, 'At least it is still there.' Very true – far easier to add more when needed, as indeed has been the case in recent times, than to start again from scratch, by which time land has likely been sold and bridges removed.

Which brings me back to my modern-day journey from Guildford to Redhill. It may not have been behind a Maunsell 'Mogul' or even in a 'Tadpole', but at least it is still possible and for that I, and I know thousands of regular travellers, can only be grateful.

Kevin Robertson

Opposite: **The down home signal at Swanwick (down trains on this east-west route were those from St Denys to Fareham) was recorded by Roger Holmes in 1973. The signal is unusual in its design, in order to give a clear sign of its indication against the background of a nearby road bridge. It would be wrong to say categorically that this type of design was unique, but it was certainly not common, and the Swanwick example may have been one of the last, if not *the* last, of its type to remain in use on the Southern Region. (Perhaps readers are able to provide information about others.) Operation here was from the station signal box, where it was lever No 2 in the frame, No 1 being the down distant and Nos 3 and 4 respectively the starting and advanced starting signals. (Lever numbers started with one of the running lines, then followed the approximate geographical layout of the track, concluding with the running signals for trains in the opposite direction.) A 200-yard track circuit was provided in advance of the signal. Your editor recalls taking a similar image around the same time, leaning over the nearby road bridge for the purpose. Mechanical signalling at Swanwick remained in operation until 9 March 1980, when the area of control from Eastleigh panel was extended.**

10

Lawson Billinton of the Brighton

Jeremy Clarke

Lawson Billinton was born on 4 February 1882, the third son and fourth child of Robert Billinton and his wife Alice, née Butzkopfski. Robert had lodged with Alice's Polish parents, when, with Stroudley's encouragement, he left Brighton – where he had been head draughtsman – to work for Samuel Johnson and the much larger Midland Railway at Derby. It is rather puzzling to know why this occurred – not that such a move was made *per se*, but why to Derby? Stroudley and Johnson had once worked together for the Edinburgh & Glasgow Railway, but had had a very uneasy, not to say rather combative, relationship. It is difficult to deduce what brought about that strong mutual dislike, though it may be because both were artists by temperament as well as engineers. Both, after all, produced aesthetically pleasing designs and clothed them in luscious liveries. One can only assume, then, that that mutual dislike did not interfere with the wider interest of giving a very promising young engineer the opportunity to gain more experience.

Robert Billinton was at Derby for 14 years before returning to Brighton as Locomotive Superintendent following Stroudley's death in 1889, filling the post of his early mentor. Hamilton Ellis suggests that David Jones of the Highland had refused it, but D. L. Bradley contends that Stroudley, foreseeing early retirement, had recommended to Samuel Laing, the Brighton chairman, that Robert succeed him.

Subsequently Lawson Billinton entered Brighton Works in January 1900 as a pupil under his father. He had already taken a course of practical and theoretical engineering at Tonbridge Technical School and subsequently obtained a mechanical engineering diploma. As was common during an apprenticeship, he moved around the shops until promoted to draughtsman in February 1903. Later that year he was promoted again, and as an inspector of materials went to Glasgow to oversee construction of some steel bogie ballast wagons. The work that followed included experimental trials with oil firing on locomotives before his next appointment as assistant foreman at New Cross, the Brighton's main loco depot in London.

Upon the arrival of Douglas Earle Marsh from Doncaster in 1905 to succeed Robert Billinton, who had died in post,

'The work of the father': 'B4' 4-4-0 No 54 is seen here decorated for a special working. Twenty-five of the type were built between 1899 and 1901, and a further nine in 1902. No 54 (seen here) was completed in May 1900, and from then until around 1912, when they were gradually superseded by the 'Atlantics' and larger tank engines, they were in charge of the principal express passenger workings, thereafter cascaded to lesser duties. The engine seen here is named *Empress*, but was renamed *Princess Royal* in August 1906. A total of 34 of the class were built, 12 of which were later rebuilt by Lawson Billinton into his 'B4X' Class. Despite the first of the type being laid aside as early as 1934, others lingered on into BR days, and No 54, by then No (3)2054 and nameless, survived on paper at least until May 1951, the same year as the final 16 were taken out of service. None is preserved.

This is No 39, one of the five Marsh 'H1' Class of 'Atlantics. According to Bradley, No 39 was for whatever reason always regarded as a 'good engine' – but not to imply that the others were in any way bad. For this reason it tended to be used for special workings and may well be seen here dutifully turned out for the special train conveying King George V to Portsmouth for the Coronation Naval Review of 24 June 1911. Two years later in June 1913, when only six weeks out from works, it was returned to the Paint Shop at Brighton Works for attention and naming *La France*, in connection with another special working carrying the President of the French Republic on an official visit. The bogie brakes fitted to the class when new were later removed.

In Southern days the class continued to work passenger services, perhaps not the immediate front-line trains of before but certainly important services including those to Newhaven, Bognor and later the Brighton to Bournemouth services. Two of the class, SR Nos 2040 and 2041, went in 1941, but the remaining three were still active after the war. No 2039, as she then was, would suffer an ignominious end, being modified by Mr Bulleid to act as his guinea pig for experiments with sleeve valves. The changes did nothing to enhance the appearance of the front end, nor indeed its reputation, and following some none too successful tests No 2039 found itself employed on the regular Lancing to Eastleigh train of carriage underframes.

In the summer of 1949, with attention now moved away from trial runs and instead concentrated on the sleeve valves fitted to No 36001, No 2039 entered Brighton Works where a replacement boiler was fitted and improvements made to the sleeve valve gear. She also emerged in plain BR black as No 32039. The intention had been for the engine to resume a normal work schedule, but for whatever reason this did not take place and instead she languished for 18 months until towed to Eastleigh for scrap in February 1951. We will never know how she performed following the improvements made to her valve gear; possibly her fate was sealed by her previous reputation as an unreliable engine (and one with considerably reduced power consequent upon the reduced diameter of the cylinders as a result of the sleeve valve fitment).

Lawson again found himself in charge of experimental business, concentrating on motor-train working and electric lighting in carriages. He was also responsible for conducting trials with Marsh's 'H1' Class 'Atlantics' on their working of heavy main-line services. Clearly Marsh was satisfied with Lawson's work as his promotion thereafter was rapid. He went first as Assistant Outdoor Superintendent at Brighton in January 1906, and a year later was back at New Cross as Assistant District Locomotive Superintendent. Five months after that he succeeded to the top post there.

At that time Brighton Works was still being reorganised with a consequent rise in the number of engines awaiting attention. Billinton relieved some of the pressure by taking several of these into New Cross for major repairs, though in truth his efforts made little impression on the overall situation. The stress on Marsh, brought about as so often by the Board abrogating responsibility for its own failures and blaming the executive and management instead, saw him granted him sick leave in February 1911, with Billinton finding himself appointed caretaker.

Billinton's brief from the Board was explicit: 'to proceed to Brighton, take general charge of the Locomotive and Carriage Works as the "locum tenens" of the Locomotive Engineer during his absence.' Among his orders was one to concentrate efforts on repair work. Marsh resigned on 1 July 1911, and although Lawson had done well during the short period in which he had been in charge, confirmation of his continuing there was questioned.

As referred to above, Marsh had for some time been making great efforts to improve the efficiency of Brighton Works through reorganisation and re-equipment. The Locomotive Committee, dissatisfied with the poor output and the costs incurred in running the Works, had in 1908 invited Robert Urie to inspect and report on the state of affairs. This must have been a rather unpleasant experience for Marsh, not simply by finding that an outsider had been brought in 'over his head', but also as Urie's arrival was at a time when the re-organisation itself had caused the already poor industrial relations within the Works to reach a particularly low point. (Marsh, it has to be said, was not the easiest of bosses, being described as having a degree of 'arrogance, impatience, obduracy and testiness'.)

Urie's report was damning, but much of the blame for the conditions could be laid upon the Board's constant refusal to authorise recruitment of more skilled men to overcome the high cost of overtime and weekend working. During one of his own battles with the Board on this subject, Robert Billinton had pointed out that it cost the company rather more to leave something like 30% of the capital loco stock standing out of service in sidings for miles around the Brighton system than it would be to repair them. Nevertheless, by the spring of 1909 Marsh's improvements and additions had begun to yield results. His successor, whoever it might be, was in a good position to take advantage of the continuing process.

Several members of the Board believed Lawson Billinton both too young and too inexperienced to succeed Marsh, and urged that Urie be invited to take over. Perhaps having obtained some knowledge through his visits of the way the Brighton Board behaved toward its officers, but more likely with the London & South Western's new Works at Eastleigh now open and in full production, Urie thanked them for their kind offer, and refused it, notwithstanding this being at a time when Drummond was still his chief at Eastleigh and not inclined to retire.

Billinton had certainly impressed several Board members in the short time he had been in charge, particularly by the inroads made into the backlog of repairs. The fact that he was a 'company man', familiar not just with its business and ways of operating but also especially with the men who would be working for and with him, enhanced the case for his appointment. His character was certainly more engaging than that of Marsh – he managed to persuade Brighton men not to join the wide-ranging rail strike of 1911 – and his engineering ability and knowledge of the relatively new science of 'time and motion', as had been demonstrated in the Works in his temporary period in charge, were taken into account. His appointment at just 29 years of age was confirmed on 18 October 1911 to commence from 1 January 1912. The principal difference in his post from that which had gone before showed late recognition by the Board that the task of 'Locomotive, Carriage & Wagon Superintendent' was now beyond the responsibility of one man to administer properly. Billinton's brief thus rested with the locomotives. Responsibility for carriages and wagons was now devolved to the very capable and long-serving A. H. Panter who, from the same date, took immediate charge of the new carriage works at Lancing in his own right rather than as a subordinate. Panter had already proved himself with some quite splendid elliptical-roofed carriages produced from 1905.

The first of the two 'J' Class 4-6-2T engines, LBSCR No 325 *Abergavenny*, was completed at Brighton in December 1910 for £3,262. Originally the engine, intended to be the precursor to a class of the same type, was allocated the number 36, later changed to 100, but appeared complete as seen. Even so, the motion parts were stamped '36'. In similar fashion, the class designation was originally shown as 'I5', but altered to 'J'.

***Abergavenny* was built with Stephenson's valve gear, whereas it will be noted that sister engine No 36 had outside Walschaerts gear. Initially coal consumption was considered heavy, but modifications to the blastpipe, dampers, ashpan and firebars, together with crew familiarity, were quick to assist. However, some problems were not so easy to deal with, including an 'unsteadiness' at speed and the 'erratic' behaviour of the bogie brakes. Tested later against the 'Atlantics', No 325 (and No 326) were better at acceleration but lacked the all-out power of the tender engines when worked hard. Bradley comments that a larger firebox and corresponding increase in grate area would likely have assisted. The tendency of No 325 to 'misbehave' at speed led to a limit of 60mph being placed for chimney-first running and 45mph when operating bunker-first. In addition, the water capacity was progressively reduced to 2,019 gallons. Billinton estimated that 2,200 gallons was the minimum required during bad weather and when steam heating might also be required. Consequently condensing gear was fitted in June 1912. (Boiler feed was by means of a Weir pump and a hot water injector.)**

Under the Southern, '2000' was added to the number and the clerestory was removed from the cab, thereby granting greater route availability. As No 32325, and by now unnamed, the engine survived into BR days and was still active on cross-country workings in Sussex and Kent, often on trains of ten or more coaches. Displaced by more modern tank engines being built at Brighton, No 32325 was withdrawn in June 1951, having accumulated 864,923 recorded miles, and was broken up a Brighton in August of the same year.

Among Billinton's first tasks on taking full charge was to complete the second of Marsh's big 'J' Class 4-6-2T engines. (There is a suggestion that had Marsh lived, many more of the class would have been produced, but, as the prototype engine was suffering teething troubles, the Locomotive Committee agreed with Billinton that just the one already started should be finished.) Construction of this second engine had begun in May 1911 but ceased a month later for work to be concentrated on six more 'Atlantics' authorised in April.

The drawings for these six had been all but completed by the chief draughtsman, Basil Field, before Marsh's departure on sick leave. (Field moved up to the post of Works Manager under Billinton.) From experience with the 'I3' Class 4-4-2T type, Schmidt superheaters were to be installed in all six. As was common practice with superheating at the time, the boiler pressure was reduced from 200psi to 170psi to the benefit of boiler maintenance. But to bring tractive effort up to about the same level, the original 19-inch cylinders were bored out to a diameter of 21 inches, fed by 10-inch piston valves. With the common cylinder stroke of 26 inches and 6ft 7½in driving wheels, tractive effort at 85% boiler pressure was 20,841lb. It should be added that Maunsell superheaters later replaced the Schmidt variety, the pressure at the same time being increased to 200psi, which raised the tractive effort to 24,518lb. This differed from the 'H1s', which at first had cylinders of a diameter of 18½ or 19 inches, giving them a tractive effort of 19,005 or 20,070lb respectively at 85% of their 200psi boiler pressure. Later all had 19-inch cylinders.

The coupled wheelbase on the 'Atlantics' was only 2½ inches greater than the diameter of the wheels, which meant that the flanges were all but touching. The boiler was of a maximum diameter of 5ft 6in and pitched 8ft 8½in above the rails, by far the largest ever to be produced at Brighton. On the 'H2' it contained – with the wide firebox, which had a grate of 30.95sq ft – 2,031½sq ft of heating surface. The superheater was of 461sq ft. Weight in working order was 68½ tons – 1½ tons more than the 'H1' – of which 37½ tons was adhesive. The tender had the usual 13-foot wheelbase, evenly divided; with 4 tons of coal and 3,500 gallons of water it weighed 29½ tons. The overall length, engine and tender, was 3 inches short of 60 feet. Billinton was able to leave his own mark on the class by tidying up Marsh's wavy footplating, add his own style of chimney and extend the cab roof back to improve crew protection. Numbered 421-6 the engines, which turned out to be the last main-line representatives of this wheel arrangement in the UK, left Brighton between June 1911 and January 1912.

The 4-4-2 wheel arrangement was, perhaps, not the ideal for the Brighton line. Marsh had at least realised that by following Ivatt's dimensions slavishly it would not provide what the Brighton needed by way of good acceleration from the more frequent station stops and the signal checks inherent in the crowded suburbs. Similarly none of the Brighton's main lines could match the long-distance hauls that characterised the Great Northern and for which the 'H1's progenitors were suited. Added to this was the fact that the routes through the Downs, especially on the Quarry line, provide some significant gradients. Neither must one overlook the initial hard work needed to combat the 30 chains or so of curve at 1 in 64 off the platform end at Victoria up to Grosvenor Bridge. Cecil J. Allen notes a non-stop run with an inauspicious start; No 421, hauling 325 tons gross, stalled on the bank on a wet and greasy rail to the extent that the train lost 11½ minutes to Clapham Junction, though 4½ minutes had been recovered to Brighton, with a maximum of 80½mph at Horley.

The second 'J', No 326 *Bessborough*, was built in March 1912 but is seen here after February 1918, at which time oval buffers and a works plate had been added. Construction of this engine had commenced at Brighton in May 1911 but was suspended in the following month while Billinton considered various changes to the design. Visibly these mainly involved the outside Walschaerts valve gear, but other alterations compared with No 325 included spiral springs and a reduced tank capacity from the outset. There was also a whistle of totally different tone. In service the outside valve gear fortunately gave little trouble, but the valves themselves were sited between the frames at the same height as the cylinders and could cause some difficulty of access when required. No 326 worked similar duties to No 325 and was similarly modified with the removal of the cab clerestory by the Southern Railway. It too was withdrawn in June 1951 having run in excess of 100,000 miles, more than its older sister. It was cut at Brighton in a very few weeks following withdrawal.

On the other hand, No 422 was once charged with taking no less than 405 tons down to the coast in the usual 1 hour from Victoria. A time of 2min 12sec to Grosvenor Road suggests that the train must have been given a hefty push from the rear for at least the length of the platform – and the Brighton-side platforms at Victoria are very long! But the engine had still lost a minute to Clapham Junction and the best part of a further minute to East Croydon. After this, time was regained slowly if surely, though a speed of 72½mph at Horley was a little less than might have been anticipated after the 8½ miles downhill from the north end of Quarry Tunnel. Nevertheless, a minute had been regained to Three Bridges and, by sustaining an excellent 50mph up to mp 31¾ at Balcombe Tunnel box, nearly another minute was won back by Keymer Junction. A final 66mph at Patcham on the run down into Brighton saw No 422 come to a stand in 3 seconds under the hour. Given the load, this was a most exhilarating run.

An up run with sister engine No 426 hauling 300 tons provides a contrasting if no less excellent showing. The train was spot on time at Keymer, passed at 74mph, before a whole series of signal checks. By the time the laggard in front had been put out of the way on to the slow lines at Balcombe Tunnel Junction, 3½ minutes had been lost by Three Bridges, but now some time recovery began. With Horley passed at 72½mph and Purley at a very unusual 75mph, the train was through East Croydon – at 55mph, well over the authorised speed limit! – only 1½ minutes down. More than a minute was then regained in the all but 6 miles to Balham and, having passed Wandsworth Common at another unusually high maximum of 71½mph, the train was nearly three-quarters of a minute early at Clapham Junction. Signals then again interfered with progress, but not so much as to prevent arrival at Victoria a quarter of a minute to the good. Allen reckons the net to have been no more than 54¼ minutes. He points out that the time of 10min 29ssec over the 10.85 miles between Purley and Clapham Junction, an average of 62.1mph, must be a rarity and, but for the final signal check, the 29.55 miles from Three Bridges to Victoria could have been made in or very close to even time.

The engines were named by the Southern and in time had the boiler mountings and the cab cut down to the composite loading gauge; even so, their excursions away from the Central Section were rare. Perhaps the furthest west they got was occasionally to Salisbury on 'through' workings to the Great Western/Western Region, though maybe the best known 'off-site' runs were with the 1950 Farnborough Air Show Specials. Air-braked stock had been borrowed from the Eastern Region but neither the Nine Elms nor Eastleigh Districts had suitable engines to haul it.

No 32421 *South Foreland* had a pleasant day out to Guildford on 6 February 1955. This was the first leg of an ambitious RCTS tour from Waterloo, the engine being in the care of an RCTS member, the late Bert Hooker. He had had no experience of the class at all other than 'prepping and disposing' them as a new recruit at New Cross Gate, and recounts that his fireman, Bill Botton, was probably the only one at Nine Elms who had actually wielded the shovel on one.

They prepared the engine at Stewarts Lane and went to Platform 12 at Waterloo via the Kensington sidings at Clapham Junction and the 'Up Windsor Local'. The route taken was through Brentford and Chertsey and the organisers approached the cab with the worrying news that they had been able to sell enough tickets to fill ten coaches rather than the expected eight. Would the engine now be capable of hauling this load up the Byfleet curve and on to the main line? Hooker assured them he'd manage. He recounts that the Addlestone Junction distant was 'on' until the engine, creeping along at about 10mph under very light steam, was some 200 yards from it. Once cleared, 'a touch of the big valve' and No 32421 jumped to it, swooping under the main line, then on to the sharply curved and steep rise to Byfleet & New Haw station. The curve and the flange drag quickly begin to take their toll but, as Bert Hooker describes it, 'she had them', all 360 tons of them, and emerged triumphantly on to the Down Slow.

In time the 'Atlantics' found themselves handling the heavy Newhaven Boat Trains, mainly because anything bigger had to go to Brighton for turning. They also had regular runs on the easily timed but sometimes heavy 'through' Brighton-Bournemouth trains, on a route that featured some difficult starts from intermediate stations west of Portsmouth, as well as services to Brighton via Lewes on the Oxted line.

The well-travelled Derek Cross recounts a footplate journey with No 32425 *Trevose Head* on the 4.40pm London Bridge-Uckfield via Oxted train, an experience he never forgot. The engine was 40 years old by this time but 'rode like a Rolls-Royce ... the best riding locomotive on which I have been' – an echo of Bert Hooker's comments on his Guildford run. Cross remarks that the firing was constant but not heavy, leaving 'a thin fire dancing on the grate and needle on the red mark all the way... I was most impressed with an old engine working a heavy train against some stiff grades.' He makes no indication of how heavy 'heavy' was, but from my personal recollection of seeing this train quite regularly at Norwood Junction in the 1950s it would have been of at least eight bogies, maybe nine, if usually Maunsell rather than Bulleid stock – say between 260 and 290 tons tare.

The 'H1s' had all gone by July 1951, and before this the first of the 'H2s' to be withdrawn was No 423, in May 1949. The rest continued until the leading bogie broke on Eastern Region 4-6-4 No 60700, Gresley's erstwhile 'Hush-Hush' engine, as it was leaving Peterborough. The bogie was repaired but, having found a flaw in the design, an inspection was made of bogies of similar pedigree. Those of the 'H2s' were among them and similar flaws were found. In view of their age it was not considered worth doing anything about the fault, meaning withdrawal. Only No 32424, the famed *Beachy Head*, was left after the other four went in August and September 1956. She lingered on in the hope, perhaps, that she might be preserved, but it was not to be and on 24 April 1958 she travelled to Eastleigh for scrap, though, game to the last, taking a train of ten coaches for Micheldever with her. Decades later, in the autumn of 2000, the Bluebell Railway announced its intention to build a replica. The basis was the fortunate discovery of a

The first 'H1', No 421, later (in 1925) named *South Foreland*, is seen in works grey and probably photographed on the Crumbles siding at Eastbourne. With the exception of the last, all of the type were built at Brighton in 1911, the final engine, No 426, taking to the rails in January 1912. Four also exceeded one million miles during their active life.

Great Northern 'Atlantic' boiler, and various other genuine and usable LBSCR parts have since been obtained. (Progress on the project can be found on the railway's website under the heading 'Bluebell Railway Atlantic Group'.)

Back in time and, with the 'H2s' out of the Works, attention turned to the second 'Pacific' tank. Billinton's main contribution here was the provision of Walschaerts outside valve gear in place of the inside Stephenson's of the older sister. Rockers were, of course, required to drive the inside valves. Less obvious was the reduction of water capacity in the side tanks and the enlargement of the well tank under the bunker as an aid to stability, and the addition of condensing gear, which required provision of a Gresham & Craven hot-water injector and a Weir feedwater pump. (Fitting these followed some obviously satisfactory experimental work on 'B2x' Class 4-4-0s Nos 171 and 317.) There were also other differences between the two: Marsh's engine had bogie brakes – removed within a short time – and laminated springs throughout, whereas Billinton's never had these brakes and was fitted with coil springs. These relatively minor differences between two very handsome engines caused the original, numbered 325 and traditionally named *Abergavenny*, to be reclassified 'J1' and the newer, numbered 326, classed as 'J2'. The latter was named *Bessborough* after the Company's Chairman, though the Brighton's number 326 had up to then usually attracted the name *Grosvenor.*

The boiler on the 'J' Classes was of 5ft 3in diameter centred at 8ft 8in above the rails. Together with the firebox, which had a grate area of 25.16sq ft, it provided 1,943sq ft of heating surface. The superheater had 342sq ft. With cylinders 21 by 26 inches and driving wheels of 6ft 7½in diameter, at 85% of Marsh's usual pressure of 170psi the tractive effort came out at 20,841lb. Coal capacity was 3½ tons, water 2,232 gallons. In working order the engines weighed 89 tons, the driving axle being the heaviest, loaded at 19¼ tons.

These were big engines for the time, handsome and speedy, and were generally allocated to working the heaviest and most prestigious Brighton services turn and turn about with the 'Atlantics' – the Pullman 'Southern Belle' for example, and the 'City Limited', with its predominance of 1st Class season ticket holders among them. Panter turned out some really superb contemporary stock for the latter service, built to the maximum of the generous Brighton loading gauge and among the few vehicles that were not dwarfed by these two engines. Though neither was at all slothful, No 326 was generally reckoned to be the faster of the two, regularly reaching more than 80mph.

The arrival of the 'King Arthurs' in 1926 (14, numbered 793-806, were built at Eastleigh with six-wheel tenders specifically for the Brighton line services) pushed the 'Js' off the best expresses, though they continued to run on the main lines until electrification began to spread from 1933. After the war they were on Oxted line services, in later days working out of Eastbourne shed on the heavily graded Cuckoo Line to Tunbridge Wells. But they could not compete with the handy 4MT 2-6-4 tank engines emerging in numbers from Brighton Works, and were withdrawn together from Brighton shed in June 1951.

Billinton had another unfulfilled Marsh order on the books, this time for ten more of the splendid 'I3s', which had taught the mighty London & North Western Railway the benefits of superheating, as well as influencing British loco design generally. He made some changes here, too, for Nos 82-91 emerged from Brighton Works between August 1912 and March 1913 with Weir feed pumps and dual braking as well as some small dimensional differences.

'I3' No 87 is seen in early Southern days before the addition of '2000' to the number, but with the 'B' prefix. It is seen at Battersea – note the 'Overhead' in the background and the Pullman vehicles in their early livery with white sides continuing to the level of the roof. The engine will be noted to be dual-braked (vacuum and air).

These engines worked primarily on the main and Mid-Sussex lines, and later to Eastbourne and Bognor until Central Section electrification from 1933 restricted their usefulness there. The class members also had their fittings and cabs cut down to the composite loading gauge, which permitted them a wider range. As with the 'Atlantics' they sometimes turned up at Salisbury in the later 1930s as well as working on the Chatham lines out of Victoria. The mainstay of their post-war years were the London-Tunbridge Wells West or Brighton via Lewes trains over the Oxted lines, and workings along the coast between Eastbourne and Portsmouth. They also had a hand in hauling the many Summer excursions to the Sussex Coast from north of the river. During the war they are reported to have appeared as far west as Gloucester and Worcester.

SR No 2082, on an east to west 'coastway' train between Brighton and Portsmouth, is seen approaching Chichester. The train has just passed the closed station at Drayton with the level crossing of the same name visible in the background.

Twenty-six of the class came to BR, only No 24 of March 1909 failing to do so, having been withdrawn in November 1944. But inroads were made from 1950 onward, and the last of this very notable class into service, No 91, was also the last out, in May 1952.

The first class entirely of Lawson's own design, the 'E2' 0-6-0 shunting tank, was built to supersede the most worn-out of Stroudley's 'E1s'. Five, numbered 100-4, were introduced in the seven months from June 1913. They had cylinders of 17½ by 26 inches, 4ft 6in-diameter driving wheels, and pressure of 170psi in the 'I2' Class boiler with which they were fitted. Tractive effort at 85% of boiler pressure was 21,307lb. The engines carried a maximum of 1,090 gallons of water and weighed 52¾ tons. Another five, numbered 105-9, came into service between May 1915 and September 1916, their introduction delayed by the onset of war. These had extended side tanks to increase the water capacity to 1,256 gallons, which added another 15cwt to the overall weight.

Though specified as shunting and local freight engines, two of them were fitted for push-pull working in 1914 and placed in the centre of six-coach trains running between London Bridge and Crystal Palace. The experiment was short-lived as the engine's bunker capacity proved inadequate. However, particularly after the Grouping, they also featured on empty stock work at the main London termini – which included drawing in and banking out the heavy 'Night Ferry' Wagons-Lits – as well as gravitating to the marshalling sidings at Herne Hill and, in wartime, to Hither Green. In the 1950s Southampton Docks saw them, up to six being allocated at any one time.

All ten received the BR '30000' and somehow as a body survived the post-war influx of diesel-electric shunters until No 108 was taken out of service in June 1961. Withdrawals that year and into 1962 saw only Nos 104 and 109 survive into 1963, and both went in April of that year.

Meanwhile Billinton had turned his attention to meeting the needs of the increasingly heavy freight movements, particularly the Continental traffic. The Directors had expressed concern about the degree of double-heading that such traffic demanded, and also that slow exits from sidings or recovery from signal checks affected the punctuality of passenger workings, particularly in the suburbs. The result was the 'K' Class 2-6-0.

The order for five at a cost of £3,150 each was made early in 1913. It is very possible that Billinton, recognising his own inexperience and keen to keep up with developments in the wider railway world, had been influenced by the success of the Churchward '4300' Class, and included a feature or two from it besides the wheel arrangement. The first 2-6-0, No 337, left Brighton in September 1913 and was followed by No 338 in December, when the trials of the prototype had proved very satisfactory. No 339 came out in March 1914, 340 in June, and 341 in November, the last appearing two months after the start of the 1914-18 War. These three engines had smokeboxes 5 inches longer than their predecessors to take account of a revised blastpipe arrangement. The earlier locos had acquired a reputation for fire-throwing and modifications had been made to counteract it. Side control of the pony trucks had also been undertaken to eliminate the rough riding reported. The measure of their success can be seen by the Government giving authority for five more to be constructed, Nos 342-6, which came into service between October and December 1916, all having the changes to the 1914 trio built in from the first.

Brand-new 'K' No 348 is also seen on the Crumbles siding at Eastbourne. The first dome was for the top feed, the pipes to which, leading to the clack valves, may be seen on either side of the boiler. This particular engine was one of those built after the First World War and was one of four that entered service in December 1920.

The boiler, provided with 1,155sq ft of heating surface, was in two rings to a maximum of 5ft 3in diameter and pitched 8ft 6in above the rails, but the most notable feature on these engines was the Belpaire firebox, quite unlike anything previously seen on the Brighton. It contained 139sq ft of heating surface and a grate area of 24.8sq ft. The Robinson superheater, consisting of unusually small 1½-inch-diameter tubes, added 279sq ft of heating surface to provide an overall total of 1,573sq ft. Pressure was originally the common Brighton one of 170psi. The big cylinders were 21 by 26 inches allied to 10-inch-diameter piston valves worked by Stephenson motion, the tractive effort being estimated as 25,103lb at 85%of boiler pressure. (In later years the pressure was raised to 180psi, boosting the tractive effort to 26,580lb.)

As with the 'J2', a proportion of the exhaust steam was fed back to the water supply through a prominent dome at the rear of the tender. Thus a hot water injector and Weir pump were needed to maintain the level in the boiler. Incidentally, the pump, mounted on the nearside footplating between the centre and rear coupled wheels, had a distinct advantage over the injector because of its ability to work at very low pressures, down to only a few pounds per square inch. The Westinghouse brake pump was mounted in the same position on the offside. Assistance to the wheel and handle reverser was provided by a compressed-air-operated clutch.

The engine in working order weighed 63¾ tons. Only 8½ tons was not adhesive, making the class very surefooted and gaining a reputation for good acceleration even with heavily loaded trains. The wheelbase worked out at 23ft 9in divided 8ft 3in + 8ft 0in + 7ft 6in. The tender was a new design with slotted frames. On its 13ft 0in wheelbase, equally divided, it carried 4 tons of coal and 3,940 gallons of water, then turning the scales at 40 tons exactly. The overall length, engine and tender, was 57ft 10in. Mechanical lubrication and steam sanding were provided. Carriage steam heating apparatus was not generally installed until after the Grouping, in part because the first call was heavy freight traffic, which didn't require it. However, most of the Brighton's stock had not been fitted with steam heating when the engines were built.

Much of the early work undertaken by the class involved moving military materials and personnel passing through Newhaven. The running of troop trains in particular showed that the engines had a good turn of speed as well as excellent power, both of which were put to good use in peacetime with the Brighton's plentiful weekend excursion traffic.

At the peak of the war years the 'Moguls' were handling goods trains of up to 1,000 tons at around 30-35mph, though the load was later set at a limit of 900 tons. It was less a matter of haulage as the ability to brake the heaviest trains satisfactorily. And though a 'K' could be turned on a 50-foot turntable the restricted site of that at Newhaven prevented this. Because of the regularity with which the class visited the shed the Board authorised construction at Brighton Works of a new 60-footer for installation at the port, completed in February 1917.

Billinton made some modifications to the class as time passed, though Nos 342-6 were fitted from new with top feed apparatus. In these cases the clacks were placed on a manhole about 3 feet ahead of the dome. Nos 337/8/40/1 received a similar modification later. No 339 was the first engine given the second arrangement, in early 1920, whereby the clacks were mounted high on the back of a second dome placed directly on the vertical centre line of the leading coupled wheels. The seven members of the class built after the war, Nos 347-53, had this style from new. The feedwater went through the clacks into a deep tray, the object being to provide 'more efficient precipitation of solids in [it]' (Marx). Boilers fitted with this second feed arrangement could also be found later on the 'B2x', 'C2x' and 'C3' classes, as well as several of the reboilered 'radial tank' classes of Billinton *père*. All were eventually abandoned for the usual positioning of the clacks on the front ring of the boiler, though the dome, where fitted, remained to cover the manhole.

With the 'J' Class engines performing very satisfactorily, Billinton decided to enlarge them to the 'Baltic' 4-6-4 wheel arrangement. It is difficult to know quite why. Electrification to Brighton was already in the air, the company's Consulting Engineer, Phillip Dawson, having been charged with investigating the possibility. As a result of his report, the South London Line between London Bridge and Victoria had 6,700V AC overhead electrification installed as much for experimental as service purposes. Electric trains ran from 1 December 1909. Electrification to Crystal Palace via Streatham Hill followed on 12 May 1911. Dawson had been charged with recommending a system suitable for electrification to the coast – here was his answer.

On another note, the 'Baltic' wheel arrangement in a tank engine had acquired a reputation for exacerbating unsteadiness with a particular penchant for rolling at speed. Billinton's 'L' Class did not do so, but it is recorded that maintenance costs on the bogies were high. Did a trailing truck as in the 'Js' have a stronger effect on the stability of an engine than a bogie? Whatever the case, two of the class were outshopped from Brighton in 1914, No 327 in April and No 328 in September. The former was named *Charles C. Macrae*. (He was a board member but also the son-in-law of the longest-serving and the most assiduous Brighton Chairman, Samuel Laing. Macrae followed his father-in-law into the top spot on the Board in 1920 at the age of 77 years.)

As to dimensions, the boiler was in two rings to a maximum of 5ft 5½in pitched 8ft 11½in above rail level. It contained 1,534.92sq ft of heating surface to which the firebox, with its grate area of 26.68sq ft, added 152.08sq ft. The superheater provided another 383sq ft. Pressure was the usual Billinton one of 170psi. The coupled wheels were 6ft 9in in diameter on a 14ft 9in wheelbase equally divided. The two cylinders set another Brighton 'first', being 22inches in diameter with a 28-inch stroke. Tractive effort at 85% of boiler pressure was estimated at 24,176lb. As in the 'J2', the 10-inch-diameter piston valves were worked by rockers from the outside Walschaerts valve gear.

Opposite: **The 'K' Class cab was left-hand drive, although the regulator could be operated from either side. The image was taken at Brighton.**

As with the GWR, and at least the LNWR (and probably others), the temptation to record the latest engine alongside one from the past was too much to resist for the LBSCR – here we see No 327 *Charles C. Macrae* alongside 'Terrier' No 682, the latter dating from 1880. Thirty-four years separated the two designs, but the smaller engine would outlive the larger and is the one that survives today.

The impressive side tanks were later made dummies after the water surging around in them affected riding. Water was then contained in a tank between the frames and another under the bunker, the main reason perhaps why the 'Ls' did not behave as alarmingly as some others of their wheel arrangement. Capacity then was 2,686 gallons, while the bunker held 3½ tons of coal.

With war now almost upon the country, production of more 'L' Class engines ceased for the moment and in 1917 Billinton was commissioned into the Royal Engineers as a temporary Lieutenant Colonel. He served mainly on railway-oriented missions in Romania and Russia. He was back home by June 1918 but returned to Romania as the head of another British Military Mission in late November, overseeing the reorganisation and reconstruction of the country's railways. Release from military service did not come until August 1919, but in the meantime he had been made CBE for this work, receiving it at an investiture at Buckingham Palace in 1920.

Note has already been made of the seven 'K' Class engines that came into service following Billinton's return to Brighton. The order was originally for ten, then seven, Nos 347-53, leaving the Works between December 1920 and March 1921. But with the Brighton's future requirements uncertain in the light of discussions between the three companies leading up to the Grouping, construction of the final three of the order was suspended. In the event Richard Maunsell decided to concentrate the 'mixed-traffic' requirement on his successful 'N' Class of 1917 and cancelled them. The view was taken that the 'N' was easier on maintenance and cost less to run. Nevertheless, Maunsell reduced the overall height of the 'Ks' to the SR composite loading gauge, though other than occasional visits to Salisbury on 'through' workings to/from the GWR/Western Region they rarely strayed from former Brighton metals.

Despite championing his own designs, anecdotal evidence suggests that the Maunsell 'N' could not match the 'K' for the steadiness of its riding, nor its ability to get smartly away with a heavy load. Not for nothing were the 'Ks' known colloquially as 'Hillclimbers'. Moreover, the class remained mechanically sound, unlike the Maunsell 'Moguls', which, as time progressed, began to show frailties such as twisted frames and cylinder failures that required several to be reconstructed.

Derek Cross relates a ride on No 350 (32350 by that time) hauling a weed-killing train on the Cuckoo Line from Polegate to Eridge. He comments that this route 'had some gradients that would make even the G&SWR men's hair stand on end! Yet the driver sat back, his pipe in his mouth, and told me the great thing about these engines was that they would not slip.' He also adds that the engine rode remarkably well, 'which may account for the fact that ... when I saw one on a relief express it seemed to be going exceedingly fast.' He further comments that 'the 'K' must rate as among the best Moguls of them all.'

At the Grouping the 17 'Ks' were concentrated at just four sheds, the bulk being at Brighton. Otherwise four were based at New Cross [Gate], two at Battersea and one at Three Bridges. On the eve of nationalisation Nos 337-47 were at Brighton, Nos 348/9 at Eastbourne, Nos 350/1 at Norwood Junction, and Nos 352/3 at Three Bridges. Three years later Eastbourne had had its allocation reduced to one, though Norwood Junction had lost its two to Three Bridges. That shed and Brighton housed seven apiece and Fratton had got hold of two.

The end for the 'K' Class came with indecent haste due to the need to reduce the number of steam engines handed over by the British Transport Commission to the British Railways Board on 1 January 1963. This followed the passing of the Transport Act 1962, which broke up the BTC into five Boards overseeing specific areas of transport, but all under the view of and (supposed!) coordination by a Minister of Transport. At the time the eight oldest 'Ks' were at Brighton, the remaining nine at Three Bridges. All 17 were withdrawn in the last two months of 1962 despite most having undergone general overhaul and/or repainting in late 1961.

Most of the withdrawn engines were stored at Brighton and Hove before sale to Kings of Norwich for breaking up. The researcher and historian Godfrey Yeomans is of the opinion that this was 'an act of politically motivated wanton vandalism'. They were certainly in a fine condition after overhaul to make that assertion valid. Yeomans rightly believed them perfectly capable of seeing out steam on BR in 1967.

It is believed that the Bluebell Railway was offered one before Messrs Kings but did not have the funds free to make the purchase. A pity, because this engine would have proved ideal on this sharply graded line, particularly now thoughts are turning to running longer and – ergo – heavier trains at times of great demand.

Billinton's penultimate 'fling' was five more 'Ls', numbered 329-333, which left Brighton between October 1921 and April 1922. The main difference between these and the first two was to be found in the boiler. The front tubeplate was recessed in by 6 inches, which reduced the total heating surface to 1,816.55sq ft. The engines weighed 98¼ tons in working order, the second and third driving axles both being loaded to 19 tons. In a reversal of Marsh's attempts to eliminate engine naming, No 329 was named *Stephenson* at the request of the Stephenson Locomotive Society. (Maskelyne reports that Billinton was far more amenable to serious naming requests than Marsh had been.) No 333 also gained a name, but under very different circumstances. She had been chosen as the LBSCR's War Memorial engine, with, according to Maskelyne, the name *Victorious*, but at the last minute someone recognised that this was not particularly appropriate in view of the engine's purpose. Moreover, and from a different viewpoint, it was clear that this would be the last engine to be built by the company. *Remembrance* she became instead. Plaques commemorating the 532 LBSCR employees who were killed during the war were attached to the side tanks beneath the name.

Billinton's last class was nominally a rebuild of his father's 'B4' 4-4-0 introduced in December 1899. In truth there was little of the original in them, only the wheel centres and bogies making the transition together with the motion and motion plate, a move that proved the valves, only 8 inches in diameter, to be the Achilles' heel of the class. The cylinders were 20 by 26 inches and the coupled wheels 6ft 9in as in the 'B4' on a 10ft 0in wheelbase, though the overall wheelbase was 2ft 4in longer than the 'B4'. The boiler, pressed at 180psi, a maximum of 5ft 3in in diameter and pitched 8ft 10in above the rails, contained 1,294.4sq ft of heating surface, of which the firebox, with a grate

The Brighton War Memorial engine, No 333, was named *Remembrance*, possibly a deliberate paronomasia as the name could also have been taken to commemorate the last steam engine to be built at Brighton, in April 1922, for the LBSCR. She is seen here for her 'official portrait' and with official war plaque. (With apologies for the 'spotting' present on the original print.)

OFFICES.
IN HONOUR OF FIVE THOUSAND SIX HUNDRED AND THIRTY FIVE MEMBERS OF THE STAFF OF THE LONDON BRIGHTON AND SOUTH COAST RAILWAY Co WHO JOINED THE FORCES OF THE CROWN DURING THE WAR OF 1914-1918 AND OF WHOM THOSE WHOSE NAMES APPEAR BELOW GAVE THEIR LIVES FOR VICTORY IN THAT GREAT STRUGGLE TO SECURE THE LIBERTY OF THE WORLD.
"THEIR NAME LIVETH FOR EVERMORE"

area of 24.8sq ft, contributed 139sq ft. Top feed was provided, though the clacks took the earlier format, being mounted on a manhole and not in a dome. The 21-element superheater had a heating surface of 279sq ft. In working order the engine weighed 58tons 1cwt with a maximum of 19tons 14cwt on the leading drivers. Tractive effort at 85% of boiler pressure was 19,644lb. The 'B4' tender was enlarged to take 3,600 gallons of water and 4 tons of coal; it weighed when full 39¼ tons.

The first of the class, No 55, came into traffic in August 1922 and was followed by No 60 in October. Both were in 'Works Grey' and never ran in the prevailing umber livery. The Southern built another ten engines up to January 1924, taking the numbers 43/5/50/2/6/67/70-3. As a class the 12 soon proved that they could not match the performance of, say, the ex-SECR 'D1'/'E1' 4-4-0s, nor indeed that of the 'I3' and 'J' Class tank engines, being noted as sluggish in acceleration and incapable of running freely. The basic problem centred around the restricted space below the cylinders, where the valves had to be fitted in, and the consequent awkward steam passages.

Like other Brighton main line engines the class found itself in limbo following electrification of the Central Section from 1933, being restricted to very secondary duties and never popular. After the war they spent much of their time in store, and as an indication of their usefulness all had been withdrawn by December 1951, Nos 2045/52/72 going together during that month.

And what of Lawson Billinton himself? It was perhaps inevitable that he would never have been seriously considered as a contender for the post of CME of the Southern. Despite his military service overseas, where he had shown willingness to don overalls and get his hands dirty, he was less experienced than either Urie or Maunsell, besides being relatively youthful. Urie declined the post because, at 69 years of age, he would be unable to serve for long, whereas Maunsell, at 54, had already proved himself a successful engineer and a particularly good administrator.

Among other things, Maunsell rebuilt the 'Ls' as a result of the electrification to Eastbourne and Hastings planned for 1935. No 329 was the first, in December 1934, and all had been through Eastleigh for the change by April 1936. The Southern classified them 'N15x', as though they were pseudo-'King Arthurs', though in truth, even if matched with a big Eastleigh bogie tender, they could not perform as that splendid class did. As Dick Hardy recounts, they could hardly move on 'first valve', but with the main one open they would hurl themselves forward, throwing fire. All seven, however, were named by the Southern at rebuilding, Nos 329 and 333 retaining their Brighton ones, the latter also keeping its plaques. The other five took the names of eminent locomotive engineers, No 332 appropriately receiving the name *Stroudley*. Incidentally, during rebuilding the cylinders had been lined to a 21-inch diameter and the boiler pressure pushed up to 180psi. Tractive effort then was 23,324lb.

After the war in general the class were based at Basingstoke and found on semi-fast passenger work on services radiating from the Hampshire town. Withdrawals were in parallel with the 'N15s', No 32330 being the first, in August 1955. *Remembrance* left in April 1956 and the class was extinct upon withdrawal of No 32331 in July 1957.

Billinton retired officially from Brighton service on 30 June 1923 – and yet not quite from the railway scene, for at the end of the 1920s he spent two years in Glasgow in a consultancy capacity for the LMS. At the Grouping he was only 40 years of age and, still active, took up fruit-growing commercially with his wife Edith (née Hilton, one of five sisters) on a 1,500-acre mixed farm at Bolney in Sussex.

Upon his second retirement Lawson Billinton moved to Haywards Heath before dying at his last home, at Lyme Regis,

Opposite and below: **As a slight digression from locomotives, here we see the unveiling of the War Memorial at London Bridge station in 1922. The heading reads 'In honour of the five thousand six hundred and thirty five members of the staff of the London Brighton and South Coast Railway Co. who joined the forces of the Crown during the war of 1914-1918 and of whom those whose names appear below gave their lives for the victory in that great struggle to secure the liberty of the world. Their name liveth for evermore.'**

on 19 November 1954, aged 72. He was a man who apparently 'enjoyed life to the full and seemed to possess an inexhaustible fund of humour and anecdote' (Maskelyne – who knew him – in his obituary). Bert Perryman, who worked with him at Brighton, concurs, describing him as 'a charming man and a great personality'. Perhaps his best memorial is the 2-inch-scale 9½-inch-gauge 'K' Class 2-6-0 No 337 that he built in his home workshop for use on his garden railway at Bolney, and believed to be still in this country. He completed and exhibited it in 1950, possibly at the Model Engineer Exhibition. It is reported that the class was his favourite.

Bibliography

The ABC of Southern Locomotives, various editions, 1942 onwards

Allen, Cecil J. *British Atlantic Locomotives* (Ian Allan Ltd, 1976)

Hamilton Ellis, C. *The London Brighton & South Coast Railway* (Ian Allan Ltd, 1960)

Gould, David *Maunsell's SR Steam Carriage Stock* (The Oakwood Press, 1978)

Bogie Carriages of the London, Brighton & South Coast Railway (The Oakwood Press, 1995)

Hawkins, Chris and Reeve, George *An Historical Survey of Southern Sheds* (Oxford Publishing Co, 1979)

Gradients of the British Main Line Railways (Ian Allan Publishing, 2016)

Hardy, R. H. N. *Railways in the Blood* (Ian Allan Ltd, 1985)

Hooker, A. E. *Bert Hooker, Legendary Engineman* (Oxford Publishing Co, 1994)

Locomotives Illustrated, No 37, 'The Larger Brighton Locomotives' (Ian Allan Ltd, 1984)

No 84, 'The Brighton Four-coupled Tank Engines' (Ian Allan Ltd, 1992)

No 105, 'The Southern "Moguls"' (RAS Publishing, 1996)

Marx, Klaus *London, Brighton & South Coast Album* (Ian Allan Ltd, 1982)

Douglas Earle Marsh: His life and times (The Oakwood Press, 2005)

Lawson Billinton: A career cut short (The Oakwood Press, 2007)

Robert Billinton: An engineer under pressure (The Oakwood Press, 2008)

Maskelyne, J. N. *Locomotives I Have Known* (Percival Marshall, 1959)

Further Locomotives I Have Known (Percival Marshall, 1962)

Moody, G. T. *Southern Electric 1909-1979* (5th ed) (Ian Allan Ltd, 1979)

Railway Track Diagrams No 5, Southern & TfL, 3rd ed (TRACKmaps, 2008)

'Table of Distances, on the London, Brighton & South Coast Railway', January 1901 (Reproduction by Ian Allan Ltd)

Welch, Michael *Sussex Steam* (Rails Publishing, 2015)

Scouring the web has obviously been undertaken to answer some questions, to confirm information from other sources or to provide pointers to possible lines of enquiry. In that regard 'semgonline' has been particularly helpful, as has Grace's Guide for further biographical detail of those people noted. I find Wiki sites can be inaccurate when data has been picked up from any other than impeccable sources, which makes it necessary to check against other information. Any inaccuracies must therefore be my own.

Salisbury to Exeter

From peak to decline and resurgence Part 1

A main-line railway

Doyen of the Southern services to the West of England was the 'Atlantic Coast Express', seen here setting out from Waterloo behind 'Merchant Navy' No 35016 *Elders Fyffes*. (The name was obviously that of a shipping line and was a subsidiary of the Elder Dempster shipping company – could we therefore say No 35016 was related to No 35030...?) As also might be gleaned from the name, the shipping line was primarily involved in the movement of bananas and other fruit, bananas in particular being imported in vast quantities on the company's vessels through Southampton Docks. The ships used were primarily freighters, but most also did have a very limited passenger accommodation. No 35016 is in early BR condition retaining the casing ahead of the cylinders and has yet to be modified with a wedge-fronted cab. We hope the coal was 'gauged' on the tender before leaving Nine Elms!

"THE ATLANTIC COAST EXPRESS"

Among the many express trains which serve Devon, one of the best known is **The Atlantic Coast Express** which runs every weekday between London (Waterloo) and the South West of England, providing morning departures in both directions.

With a Refreshment Car to and from Exeter (Central) **The Atlantic Coast Express** covers many parts of Devon as it has Through carriages which branch off after Exeter to Ilfracombe, Torrington and Plymouth, as well as to Seaton, Sidmouth and Exeter.

This train, as its name implies, of course, has a portion for Cornwall, too.

TO AVOID DISAPPOINTMENT IT IS ADVISABLE TO RESERVE SEATS ON THIS EXPRESS AS WELL AS MANY OTHER DUPLICATE TRAINS

The 88 miles of railway from Salisbury to Exeter formed the bulk of the 'Main Line to the West' of the former LSWR and SR systems and indeed for the early years under BR ownership, that is until rationalisation and associated contraction took place around the mid-1960s.

We have for a long time wanted to describe in detail the build-up to this closure and consequential operation of what was for some a cross-country backwater, starved of investment and left to survive as best it could. Here in the first of what will be several separate parts we look first at how the railway came into being, its peak, including mention of the lines radiating into and connections from it, through the glory times and thence to the start of the 1960s and the boundary changes that almost spelled the end of the Salisbury-Exeter line as a through route. To achieve this was no easy task and at the start I would state that we have been ably assisted by Jeffery Grayer and Michael Upton, without whose expertise and involvement this piece could never have been written.

Back in the middle of the 19th century attempts to reach Exeter and beyond by rail from London were in the competitive hands of the Bristol & Exeter/Great Western and London & South Western companies. The B&E was worked by the GWR and, while not formally absorbed as part of that company until the 1870s, it may be convenient for the purpose of this narrative to refer simply to the GWR and LSWR routes.

By means of the GWR, the railway reached Exeter from London in 1844, creating a line running via Bristol some 194 miles long and for many years leading to the initials GWR being interpreted as 'Great Way Round' – which, to be fair ,it was. (Interestingly, today some West of England trains still reach Exeter [and beyond] travelling via Bristol. Indeed, your author can confirm that some modern-day services still [or did] take the same route at certain times of the day – even, as in my experience, venturing via Weston-super-Mare south of Bristol.) By comparison, the LSWR route as built provided a geographically more direct route of 171½ miles. (A more direct route for the GWR, travelling via Westbury following the opening of the various 'cut-offs' at Westbury, Frome and Langport, reduced the 194 figure to a more competitive 174 miles.)

A third rail route between London and Exeter might also have come about had the desires of Charles Castleman, a Wimborne solicitor, come to fruition. At the time when the LSWR, under the guise of the its original title of the London & Southampton Railway, had just reached Southampton, Castleman proposed a westwards extension through the New Forest to Ringwood, Wimborne (not perhaps unnaturally), Dorchester and eventually on to Exeter via Bridport.

The history of this enterprise is ably covered in the two volumes produced by The Oakwood Press series on 'Castleman's Corkscrew' by Brian Jackson. For the present, suffice to say that the term 'Corkscrew' came about due to the circuitous nature of the line, especially between Brockenhurst and Poole, while the terminus at Dorchester faced west as if reaching out to what would hopefully be the Exeter extension. It would never be – Castleman, realising his limitations, attempted to interest the LSWR in continuing his scheme, but was rebuffed in favour of an extension west from Salisbury. With a connection later made at Dorchester into the GWR's Wilts, Somerset & Weymouth line by means of a south-facing chord, the legacy was for many years a through platform at what was Dorchester (South) for down trains only, all up services running past this platform before reversing into what was then designated the up platform, an unsatisfactory arrangement that curiously persisted until as late as 1970. Concluding this part of our story, the LSWR later built a cut-off from Brockenhurst on a more direct path to reach Christchurch (and so on to Bournemouth), after which the original 'Castleman's Corkscrew' route via Wimborne quickly fell into the category of a secondary line. It would close in 1966.

With the growth of motor vehicle traffic and consequential road building in the late 20th and into the 21st century it is interesting to note that the three principal road routes between London and Exeter are similar in many ways to the corresponding rail routes, extant and proposed. By road using the M4 and M5 (travelling thus via Bristol) the distance is 197 miles (194 by rail). Following the Southern route close to Salisbury the road distance is 173 miles using the M3 and A303 (171 by rail), and via the south coast, M3, M27, A31, A35, it is 183 miles. For the latter there is no direct rail comparison, as the A35 takes the traveller via Bridport, the proposed rail route that was never built. To the motorist each has it advantages and equally its disadvantages.

So we return to the original thrust of this article and the railway west of Salisbury, which opened in two parts: Salisbury to Yeovil on 2 May 1859 (1 June 1860 to passengers) and thence from the latter point on to Exeter on 19 July 1860. Gradually branch lines and connections into other parts (or related to our story) were made as follows:

Warminster (from Westbury to Salisbury), part of the GWR Wilts, Somerset & Weymouth lines – 30 June 1856

Salisbury Market House – 24 May 1859

Exmouth branch – 1 May 1861

Yeovil, connection to Yeovil Town – 1 June 1861

Templecombe, connection to the Somerset & Dorset system – 1862(?)

Exeter Queen Street-Exeter St David's (connection between the LSWR and GWR) – 1862

Chard branch – 8 May 1863

Seaton branch – 16 March 1868

Sidmouth branch – 6 July 1874

Lyme Regis branch – 24 August 1903

Fovant Military Railway – 15 October 1915

With the railway open, through services could begin, and not just trains to Exeter, for as the LSWR influence grew west of

From that master of photography George Heiron we see No 34051 *Winston Churchill* entering Salisbury station with a down (westbound) train. (It is strange that the nameplate was not later changed to reflect the great man's knighthood. Does any reader have an idea why? Such changes to plates were certainly made on other company engines, notably on the GCR and GWR.)

34051
10
S. R.
PASSENGERS
MUST CROSS LINE
BY BRIDGE

Two new (we believe) views of the disaster at Salisbury of 1 July 1906. The cause (speed) and circumstances of the accident are well known, and are one of the reasons why even today there are no booked through passenger trains that run non-stop through the station. Indeed, I think I am right in saying that the only service that ever did so in more recent years was the 'Devon Belle', notionally non-stop from Waterloo to Exeter, but which paused at Wilton for an engine change in either direction. (The reader is also referred to the excellent 'South Western Circle' monograph on this disaster.) *Denis Calvert*

Exeter the outcome would be through workings beyond Exeter, culminating in London to Plymouth services via Salisbury, Exeter and Okehampton. There were also through services to Plymouth originating from Brighton.

Geographically the railway between Salisbury and Exeter was very much of a switchback nature, especially beyond Semley where there exist long stretches at gradients as steep as 1 in 80, the majority of them against down trains. Indeed, the changes of level occurred so often that the majority of the stations en route could not be built on sections of level line, requiring great care to be exercised to avoid runaways when shunting or when attaching/detaching vehicles.

As opened, the new railway west was a combination of both single and double lines but, as with many builds, an eye to the future had seen much of the formation and bridgework able to accommodate a second line of rails, which was indeed completed throughout by 1867. It was somewhat ironic that a century later the wheel would literally turn full circle in this area. Initially signalling was rudimentary to say the least, although by 1875 new signal boxes had opened throughout from Salisbury west.

Train services

According to Bradshaw of October 1897, there were westbound departures at intervals starting at 8.20am and continuing through the day until 7.57pm. Principal among these were the 1.05 and 4.54 afternoon trains from Salisbury, each making just one stop en route to Exeter, respectively at Templecombe and Sherborne. The journey time was in the order of 2 hours on these 'fast' services, or a little over 3 hours if the train stopped at all stations. On Sundays there was just one through service; leaving at 2.00pm, it took a desultory 3½ hours or more for the 88 miles to Exeter stopping at all stations and achieving a less than startling average speed in the order of 25mph.

There were more departures in the up direction, although some of these would only venture as far as Yeovil. Two were designated fast trains, one a morning service from Exeter Queen Street, arriving at Salisbury in 2 minutes under the 2 hours, inclusive of a 7-minute wait at 'Templecombe Junction' (sic). The second 'fast' service made four intermediate stops and took a shade over 3 hours for the same journey – perhaps the word 'fast', which appeared in the timetable against this train, was subject to

From the Edward Wallis archive we have this view of Crewkerne, looking east on 17 April 1934. Edward Wallis was not a man to record trains, preferring instead to concentrate on infrastructure and especially signalling. The gradient on the main line is obvious compared with the level of the sidings. Indeed, the whole railway between Salisbury and Exeter was very much a switchback over which Cecil J. Allen once remarked the Bulleid 'Pacifics' would 'gallop'. That, of course, would be a few years ahead of when the view was taken, with Crewkerne, like many of the other stations on the line, seeing as many non-stop services as they did stopping trains.

liberal interpretation at Waterloo! The last weekday train from Exeter Queen Street, by which it was possible to reach Waterloo, left the Devon city as early as 6.00pm, after which it was possible to go to Salisbury only by the 6.05pm. After this, a Salisbury or London passenger would find himself unceremoniously tipped out on to the platform at Templecombe. As in the down direction, on Sunday there was just one train traversing the complete length of the line.

Forty years later, in the summer of 1937 the service had become far more intense. The first down train, for example, left Salisbury (from Waterloo) at 2.32am and was a through train to Ilfracombe, calling only at Yeovil Junction before its next stop at Exeter. Arrival there was not until 5.05am, inclusive of a 28-minute wait at the intermediate stop. There might well have been two reasons for this delay. First, a stopping service originating from Eastleigh left Salisbury at 2.48am and called at various intermediate stations before arriving at Yeovil Junction while the Ilfracombe service was still at the platform. Possibly it then afforded a connection to Ilfracombe, and other 'west of Exeter' routes to passengers from intermediate points without the need to stop the main train at numerous stations on the way. The other reason was that there was really little point in a fast service depositing passengers at their destination when there was nothing open; certainly the ladies in their boarding houses would hardly welcome a traveller at that time. Even so, it was still a 7.29am arrival time at the destination, having taken just over 7 hours from Waterloo – this, remember, without sleeping car accommodation being available. (There was no corresponding night train from Exeter to Waterloo.)

Services proper started at 8.05am. and as this was the summer timetable various other through and restaurant car trains were specifically referred to. The timetable makes particular mention of 'Through Restaurant Car Waterloo to Sidmouth (...Seaton...Exmouth)' – three separate trains, of course. Then there were the three timetabled portions of the 'Atlantic Coast Express', departing from Waterloo at 10.35, 10.40 and 11.00am. All three had identical stopping points, i.e. just Salisbury and Exeter Central, yet by the time they had reached Salisbury these three trains had already become increasingly separated, ever more so by the time Exeter was reached. There was also a better service into the evening. The summer Saturday service is best described as 'intense', with line capacity at a premium and of course based upon trains keeping to time hauled by willing crews with engines able to keep to the schedule. There were also only limited places where it was possible to overtake a slower running service without having to resort to a 'wrong-road' move (i.e. when a slower service was shunted on to the opposite line to allow a faster service heading in the same direction to pass – Seaton Junction and Yeovil were the most obvious locations). Just one delayed or poor running train could potentially have a knock-on effect for the rest of the day's service. Sunday again witnessed a greater service than in the previous century, through trains west starting at 10.00am and running until 9.00pm, although it should be said that there were also a number of shorter-distance workings, starting from Salisbury as well as intermediate points en route, Yeovil Junction and Sidmouth Junction being two examples.

In the opposite direction there was a corresponding number of workings – after all, what goes up must come down, or, to be more accurate, what goes down must come back up. Interestingly the restaurant car workings are shown as 'From Exeter', meaning that the various destinations served by such vehicles on the way down did not benefit from a similar arrangement for the reverse. Might this have been the mere practicalities of restocking said vehicles? Presumably Exeter was a victualling site, but one could hardly have expected the same stores to be available at Seaton, Sidmouth or Exmouth. (Perhaps a knowledgeable reader could describe the carriage workings for such vehicles...)

The summer timetable (weekdays and Saturdays) for 1964 ('15 June to 6 September', Table 35 in the public book) reveals a similar although not identical number of trains compared with before the war. There is still a down overnight service from Waterloo, but it is now shown as 'Through carriages to Ilfracombe and Plymouth'. Later in the morning there were just two portions to the 'ACE', while with one exception (to Yeovil) all mention of restaurant cars is to say that they only run to Exeter and not the various branch line termini. Dependent upon demand, 'relief' trains were still a feature of the period, provided there was a locomotive, crew, rolling stock and pathway available. These would be arranged at short notice, often in consequence of the Traffic Inspector at Waterloo seeing an increasing rather than a diminishing crowd after the departure of a train such as the 'ACE', although relief workings for other destinations were similarly provided, again dependent upon the above criteria. Contact was then made with Control, which in turn would speak to Motive Power and, all being well, a train could be conjured up in a relatively short space of time. It was just accepted that passengers might have to wait, and they did. Perhaps we were all somewhat more enduring in years past.

In addition to the passenger workings there was of course freight (more accurately non-passenger services) between Salisbury and Exeter, although this was mainly in one of three categories. First there were trains of ballast from Meldon to all parts, the working of these heavy trains being irregular and for many years usually in the hands of an 'S15'. As these were invariably a long and slow pull, it required some planning to ensure locations such as Honiton bank could be surmounted, then a refuge made further on without undue delay to an up passenger train following. For this reason such trains could also be run at night. Next we should consider the regular 'non-passenger' but also 'non-freight' trains in the form of milk. Some came all the way to London for Vauxhall or Morden, but others were dealt with at places such as Seaton Junction or Chard. In the up direction the heavy tanks were run at some speed and again had to be slotted into the existing service, while a main-line engine was invariably used for the return empties. Finally there were the pick-up freight services that served the intermediate stations, often a daily service but one that might be curtailed at short notice to give priority to extra passenger trains as well as releasing both locomotives and crews for the same purpose. En route there would also be interchange of traffic at Templecombe and Yeovil. Slotted into all of these were 'Q' paths (pathways available for special workings), which could include an additional passenger or perhaps a livestock train or an empty stock movement.

From April 1950 regional boundary changes saw the Southern lose control of its lines west of Exeter, the so-called 'Withered Arm'. This in itself might not have been too bad – after all, for some years past Waterloo had joked that it would have been a lot better off if they could have persuaded Paddington to take over these lines in the quieter months. But the difficulty was that Paddington now had control for 12 months of the year and a relationship that depended upon a continuation of through 'inter-regional' workings was not one that bode well for the long-term future. Matters became more difficult when in 1963 the WR went one stage further and was now responsible for the route from the former SR station at Wilton all the way to Exeter. Worse was to follow in the shape of the Beeching Report. Closure of branch lines, closure of intermediate stations and a seemingly ever-changing view from 'the Kremlin' (as 222 Marylebone Road was wont to be known) as to whose route might be retained, developed or even slated for closure. It was a sad and fateful period for those BR managers forced to implement change on the ground, both to railway staff and the travelling public. One example may be given when the WR announced that Yeovil would no longer be given the status of a stopping place on through Exeter to Waterloo trains and passengers should instead make their way to neighbouring Sherbourne or travel via local services to Westbury and change trains there. A barrage of protest followed and Yeovil retained its status.

But at what cost? The railways were losing money, and each closure or rationalisation might have saved money on paper, but the knock-on effect does not appear to have been calculated. A branch line no longer providing a few passengers for the main line, a curtailed service now calling at every station and so taking longer – it was impossible to calculate the financial impact on passenger numbers, and consideration of any social impact was not in the equation at the time.

One of the casualties of rationalisation was Seaton Junction, seen here in September 1928 freshly rebuilt and expanded, yet half a century later it would all be closed and just a single line of rails would remain. In happier times, looking west, we see here the station with up and down loops leaving the running lines free for non-stop services. The branch to Seaton had its own bay platform, trailing in on a curve beyond the concrete footbridge (one of the longer products of that type produced by the Exmouth Junction concrete works and still standing today). The tall lower-quadrant signals (the up starting signals) remained in use until the end, a magnificent example of the signal engineer's art. The co-acting arrangement was necessary to give the driver of an up train sufficient warning of the state of the line as he approached at speed on the long descent from Honiton Tunnel. The Southern Railway never operated slip coaches on the former South Western lines (Gordon Weddell imparts some limited information concerning slip coaches on the LSWR, but not their workings, on p91 of the Oakwood Press title *A History of Slipping and Slip Coaches*), but had it done so, this would surely have been the perfect spot for such a service. (More views of Seaton Junction and indeed the SR in the period 1922 to 1934 may be found in the two *Southern Railway Infrastructure* titles featuring solely images from the Edward Wallis collection.)

So economy was the order of the day and, as we know, long sections of single track became the norm, with crossing loops at intervals, but in the process limiting the timetable. Freight had by now also all but disappeared, although ballast and, for a little while yet, milk was still moved. There would be changes in motive power as steam receded from the scene and, as might be expected, signalling as well, these being the subject of future articles in this series.

Why it was all necessary? The simple reason was money. To fund investment elsewhere, the railway had to be seen to be saving money in its loss-making areas. This was the remit passed by Government to the British Railways Board, and in turn cascaded to the regions.

What really comes out of this very brief look at the period leading up to the changes of the 1960s is how alterations to regional control would start to have a detrimental effect on the service, accelerated by local closures and the additional complication of alterations to motive power. We might even say that some of what transpired occurred due to a lack of resources and rationalisation, with closure being the easiest option. For the Salisbury-Exeter line to succeed as a through route, albeit seeming to be a cross-country backwater, there also needed to be cooperation between the controlling/operating regions. Paddington and Waterloo, though, had their own ideas and priorities; Waterloo, for example, planned diesel depots in the South West to service a fleet of SR DEMU sets operating the branch lines, while around the same time Paddington sought to stave off attempts to single its West of England cut-off route from Westbury to Taunton. Considering the latter especially, why should the WR then make any effort to save a competing line to the west via Salisbury?

One feature of the line west of Salisbury that has not been mentioned but should be was the principally rural terrain through which the railway ran, which was therefore unlikely to yield much in the way of traffic, although we should not forget milk at Seaton Junction and Chard Junction, together carpets from Axminster. Otherwise it was a railway of interchange points: Templecombe and Yeovil, intermediate branches to the destinations already described, and primarily holiday traffic. To the Southern Railway, its predecessor and the first decade and more of BR, this was perhaps acceptable even if it did mean coaching stock standing idle for more months than they were active. If it could have been seen, the seeds of demise were thus already sown. The Southern and its marketing policy together with the romanticism associated with long-distance train travel typified, we must say, by such names as the 'Atlantic Coast Express' had unwittingly created a business that was hardly year-round dependable. It was this very weakness that would come to be exploited in the years to come.

Other articles in this series will feature 'Salisbury-Exeter: 30 years of change, 1963-93 – Infrastructure', 'Salisbury-Exeter: 30 years of change, 1963-93 – Motive Power', and 'Salisbury-Exeter: From absolute block to tokenless block – a new signalling system'.

The loco-hauled era: gone are the days of steam, while the 'Warship' days are similarly but a memory. After this time the SR/WR agreed to try Southern Class 33 diesels, but they proved to be underpowered and it was perhaps fortunate that Class 50 machines, themselves displaced from the WR in consequence of the influx of the HST sets, were now available. Until their own replacement by modern day DMU sets, the Class 50s were therefore the mainstay of passenger services, Mark 2 stock also having replaced the earlier Mark 1 coaches with the whole now coming under the 'Network SouthEast' banner. Honiton in the 'South East'? *Jeffery Grayer*

Life at Eastleigh in the latter days of steam
Part 2

John Stubbington

I mentioned last time about some of the characters of the old railway. Well, there were many, each with his peculiarities. One particular driver, for example, would always arrive either just on time or a few minutes late, understandably perhaps if it was a very early start but less easy to appreciate if the shift began at a more reasonable hour. Others were always there early. Similarly some drivers would help the fireman, others would not. I quickly worked out who were the best to be with – not that I had a lot of choice of course – but a good one would help the fireman, perhaps by checking the smokebox door was tight as he went around, and I in return might assist with the oiling, which was officially the driver's responsibility.

District Motive Power Superintendent Stephen Townroe's photograph shows the office block and coaling stage at Eastleigh in the 1950s. The locomen's signing-on point and lobby were accessed under the canopy, while the 'Enquiries' sign was identical to that which might be seen on a passenger platform. Not a 'Pacific' in sight either, instead an 'N15', 'Lord Nelson' and a 'Q1' with something else unidentified at the far end – a 'K' perhaps? Townroe had the bulk of the 'Lord Nelson' Class transferred to Eastleigh during his tenure specifically for working the boat trains from Southampton Docks. Having many crews thus becoming truly familiar with the type, together with their mannerisms, enabled a far more reliable performance on such services.

With a good driver, if I arrived first, when my mate did turn up he would likely say, 'Everything all right, nipper?' I would say 'Yes', because I knew the routine. It was all part of a ritual, the same ritual regardless of the engine, the duty or the time, or even the actual conditions. If there were problems, they would come out as we prepared/worked together, often finding things were never really as bad when they were shared. When all was eventually ready and the driver had settled down – this was usually the time he rolled a cigarette, in itself an important part of the ritual – we would be off, and not before. No amount of cajoling, shouting or threats from a foreman made anyone move any faster than they felt was comfortable. Not that anyone did – each man knew his allotted task and simply got on with it.

I can say it now – bearing in mind I was only 16 at the time – that these men were (to me) old and I considered them to be (at least) 60 plus, although in reality they were probably only in their forties!

THE
CUNARDER
SPL

I recall the characteristics of one particular driver, although unfortunately not his name, who was always smart, well turned-out in appearance, shiny boots, collar and tie, and all his badges clean too. He carried a pocket watch, as many men did in those days, and had the particular habit of checking the time quite frequently both on the road and elsewhere. Known for this, some drivers would look to see if he had just checked his watch, then deliberately ask him for the time. The fact that he had just looked was of no consequence, and he would dig in his pocket and check it again; obviously doing this was a habit that he had done for years and no doubt based on years of having to ensure that the service he was working ran to time.

Another very smart, well turned-out fireman was Charlie Marsh. He was in the main-line gang, which would require him to fire on the fast trains between Waterloo, Basingstoke, Winchester and Southampton. Any other fireman would get off the footplate quite grubby, but not so Charlie. His face would be clean, his very pale blue, almost white, overalls pristine, his British Railways cap badge gleaming. He also had a permanent smile on his face. How he managed it I cannot imagine, as to be sure he would certainly have had his share of poor engines, coal and the like. Looking back I should certainly have asked him his secret.

I recall one shift, a night turn, when I was mated with a rather bad-tempered driver by the name of Cyril Wilkins. I learned later that he was not always the same, but for whatever reason I caught his wrath that night. We had a 'Q1' destined for Salisbury hauling a heavy freight and travelling via Chandlers Ford. The route from Eastleigh was a gentle climb nearly all the way. Well, it was 2.00am and I was having a problem making this one steam. So bad did it get that there was a real risk that the engine's brakes would come on as we passed Dean Hill sidings between Dunbridge and Dean stations at little more than walking pace. Without warning Cyril jumped up from his side of the cab and pushed me aside, at the same time shouting, 'Boys like you ought to be at home in their beds!'

With that he grabbed one of the fire irons and furiously stoked up the fire, to regain steam. With hindsight perhaps he was indeed right and I was wrong, but in my defence I would say I was only 16 and did not have the years of experience he had amassed. But it might have been better if he had tried to guide me earlier, when he could clearly see that things were not going well. Whatever, his action was in fact timely, enabling us to get over the hill at Dean. Phew, it was now downhill through Laverstock and into Salisbury station, where we were relieved by another crew ready for the train to continue its way west.

In the same direction I recall being on the goods turn to Romsey, where we would be employed shunting for several hours. For whatever reason, I remember there was often a large amount of animal feed on these turns, carried in closed vans.

Chichester was the location of another story. Booking on at 10.00pm, my driver and I had about a 2½ hours to wait before we had to depart. (I do not recall if this was usual or if we were advised our train was running late on that particular occasion.) With a long wait pending, my driver told me he was off to a 'local' he knew. No problem so far – I spent the time doing what I liked doing, looking at engines. Come the time when we had to leave, the train had arrived but not my driver. I began to get worried as this was a situation I had not experienced before. What to do? Make myself scarce as well, tell someone and likely get him and perhaps also me in trouble, or just hope he would arrive soon? Fortunately it was the latter and he arrived without a care in the world just before further action was likely to have been taken to get the train moving on time.

One turn that I did enjoy was the 4.30pm Southampton Terminus to Bournemouth Central stopping passenger service, unusual perhaps for me in the lowly link I was in, but I was not going to object. We called at all stops, and since by now I had a regular driver he allowed me to do the driving, every boy's dream. Usually it was a tank engine with about four coaches on and timed to pick up working people to get home.

My driver had also got used to the fact that when I was firing I was left-handed. Most of my mates were OK with this, but if I was with a different driver I made sure to tell him beforehand, especially if the engine we had was right-hand drive, as were some of the members of the 'U' Class.

Right: **John stands alongside a withdrawn 'Schools' at Eastleigh in 1962, the number of which was not recorded. The end of the 'Schools' came about simply due to the need to reduce the number of classes of steam traction, although by then many of their duties had already been deputed to BR 'Standard' types. Speaking to other Eastleigh men from the same period, and notwithstanding that they were just a 'tool that they used', some appeared genuinely sad to see them go.**

Opposite: **An unidentified member of the 'Nelson' clan stands outside Eastleigh shed carrying the headboard of a boat train. John never worked one of these trains but does recall firing a 'Nelson' on mail trains to and from Basingstoke as well as later being the second man on a Class 33 that was hauling the preserved member of the class, No 30850.** *Les Elsey*

On the road, one of the many jobs that a fireman had was to keep an eye on signals and anything else that the driver might not be able to see from his side of the cab. The driver's side, usually the left, had a very restricted view ahead, taking account of the length of the engine. This was made even more difficult when running in reverse. Another, perhaps obvious, task was to make sure that there was enough water in the boiler, just as important as having enough steam at the right time to make the engine move and so haul its train.

As will be gathered, every engine was different to work on. They all had the same working functions, so the driver's controls were constantly the same, but not always in the same place! No two engines would behave the same either, even members of the same type, while it was the fireman who would have to deal and cope with a bad steaming engine, like the one I mentioned earlier going to Salisbury. Another in the 'not very nice' category was tender-first running in the pouring rain on an engine not steaming and with a surly driver. Yuk – surely there must be a better way of earning a living!

Obviously we worked around the clock in terms of hours of attendance, and personally I hated things like a 3.30am start. This was not helped by the fact that in nearly every other job there was a set finishing or 'end of shift' time. Not so on the footplate – you finished when you got back to shed, perhaps having been delayed by any one of a number of reasons. Using the 3.30am start as an example, and bearing in mind that I was 16, I naturally wanted a social life. Instead I would have to get up by 2.30am to cycle to the shed and, if I was lucky, finish by 12 noon, then cycle home and back to bed until perhaps 5.00pm – that is if it was possible to sleep with the sounds of the day all around. Later it was up and out, as one would with your mates, until the need to get to bed for a few hours again before getting up once more at 2.30am. No surprise that after a week of this I was very tired.

Soon afterwards came what was probably my most memorable ever footplate experience. I had been booked 'spare' that morning, meaning I was waiting in the 'cabin' (the room where all the spare drivers and firemen congregated ready to cover a man who had perhaps not arrived, a turn where the crew had been delayed, or to work a short notice special train). In came Cyril Legg, the shift foreman. He looked at me, beckoned and said, 'Nipper, get yourself down to Bournemouth West.'

I learned later that the booked fireman for none other than the 'Pines Express' was not available; I never found out why, and Bournemouth depot had no one available to cover the turn. Obviously they had enough notice to advise Eastleigh, hence the request. Thinking back, what was also strange was why I was chosen. There were probably more senior men available, but it was me who had been told, so I simply went – travelling 'on the cushions' by the next service train to Bournemouth.

At Bournemouth West the train was already standing in the platform with No 34105 *Swanage* at its head. 'Thirteen on,' said the driver, all Mark 1 coaches in maroon livery. What a baptism, and certainly my first time on a train of such importance. The route was via Oxford as, despite the name, the service had already been diverted away from its previous route using the Somerset & Dorset line to Bath.

At Bournemouth shed on 9 August 1966 there is no No 34105 unfortunately, but instead Nos 34037 *Clovelly*, 80085 and 34066 *Spitfire* are present, together with a vehicle from the breakdown train. In the background is the wheel hoist and the water softener. Some attempt has been made to clean the side of the tank engine, the difference showing just how dirty things had become. *Tony Harris*

Class 4 No 76018 arrives at Portsmouth & Southsea with a parcels train in the late summer of 1966. In the background one of the ubiquitous 4-COR sets waits to form a main-line service. Portsmouth & Southsea signal box is also visible. *Tony Harris*

So there I was at 16, ready for work on this prestige train that I would be responsible for firing as far as Basingstoke, so I was told, and a fair chunk of that uphill. I remembered the time when, as a child, I had written to Hornby asking them to please produce a model of the class. No need now – I was on the real thing.

There was little time to look around, although I did notice that the fire was bright and burning and the water well up in the boiler. Someone had got her ready, and she was just right. I remember the guard blowing his whistle and with an answering call on the engine whistle by the driver we were off for our first stop at Bournemouth Central. A bit of wheel slip and, with the fire roaring away as a result of the exhaust, I began shovelling away for all I was worth.

I always felt that the Central station at Bournemouth had an almost cathedral-like appearance as a result of its high roof, but there was little time to admire the view before we were off again, next stop Southampton Central. I assume we kept time, whatever that was, and it was certainly not hard work all the way as I was able to enjoy the view through the New Forest, passing Christchurch, Brockenhurst, Totton and the like before coming to a stop at the London end of Platform 1, exactly right for water as well. (This was where a driver proved his worth; going was easy, but stopping on the exact spot was a skill, especially when the back of the tender had to be positioned just right so the water column could be reached. I expect my driver had a 'spot' or mark he gauged by. Whatever, he was right on – you certainly cannot pull forward or ease back for another go with all the carriage doors open.)

As soon as we stopped, I was up on the tender to put the 'bag' in it, after which I jumped over into the coal space and began to push as much coal forward as I could, which would be to my advantage once we got moving again. This process took about 10 minutes. It is uphill all the way to Basingstoke and I would be shovelling coal nearly all the time. In the meanwhile the driver was dealing with his 'bits', probably checking around the engine, although, to be fair, so engrossed was I with my own tasks that I hardly noticed what he was doing. I did see that the platform was full of people, some of whom might well have been travelling the entire way to the final destination at Manchester Central.

Once the coal had been brought forward I was back on the footplate, building up the fire again. The driver accepted the guard's whistle and green flag, as they were on his side, and after a quick check to confirm that the starting signal was in the 'off' position we were on the move. We passed the advanced starting signal (also clear) and were immediately into the dark cavernous tunnel underneath the streets of Southampton. Immediately the smoke and steam from the accelerating engine billowed into the cab, the whole illuminated by light from the firebox as I continued with the shovel.

Towards the far end there was a bend to the left, but not enough to prevent some light from outside to be seen, and we were soon on the sharp curve taking us to Northam Junction and past the signal box of the same name with its large 56-lever frame. Once all our train was on straight track again we could start to accelerate, passing Mount Pleasant Crossing and approaching St Denys, where I remember the driver blowing the whistle again. As speed increased ever more, we passed Swaythling, then the site of my early trainspotting days at Stoneham. As we reached Eastleigh our speed was around 65mph and I gave myself a break from shovelling as we passed underneath Campbell Road bridge, the one that I used to stand on with my bike, years earlier. Passing Eastleigh West signal box on our left, we took the up fast line, whistling as we gained even more speed. I rested my aching arms on the wooden window frame to see who I could see on the platform! And ... there was not a soul to wave to!

Never mind, I remembered what I had been tasked to do and concentrated on my duties until we came to a stand at Winchester City. Unlike at Southampton Central, I now had time to exchange words about how it was all going. The driver was happy, so great! Within a few minutes we were away again, still climbing all the way and through the various tunnels at Wallers Ash, Micheldever and Popham, the last signifying that it was now downhill all the way to Basingstoke, except for the brief climb over the West of England main line at Battledown flyover.

Approaching Basingstoke we reduced speed. No 34105 had performed well, so well that I did not want to get off. Slowly running through the platform, there was the characteristic clanking sound of the motion echoing under the canopy, becoming ever less as we slowly come to a stop. Here an Oxford crew was waiting, giving me some slightly strange looks, no doubt on account of my youth. It was back to earth with a bump as the driver and I travelled back 'on the cushions', with me of course getting off at Eastleigh. Probably a unique experience for a 16-year-old.

This story was unusual in another way, as I had a driver from another depot. Normally you had the same driver for one week or even several weeks, and could thus build up a good working relationship. As time passed the knowledge between you and the driver resulted in the bonding of a team. If there was trust, after some time the driver might also get you to do the driving. Now that was another dimension of the job and one that I had thought much about at the start. It also meant that with the driver doing the firing, he was also keeping his hand in should he need to do so, and it really was a marvellous feeling to drive a steam engine, be it for a journey to Bournemouth from Eastleigh, or just from Eastleigh depot to the shunting yard!

Time (and electrification) marches ever on. Class 5 No 73018 with a Bournemouth line working pauses at Basingstoke's Platform 2, with a noticeable replacement number plate. By this date, 13 August 1966, the engineers were pushing further west all the time and plans had even been made for the electrification of the Alton line to Winchester. In the event these were not proceeded with due, so it was said, to lack of materials. Privately, certain engineers admitted that so much over-ordering had taken place with reference to the main line that there was probably enough to equip the Alton road or at least a fair proportion of it! *Tony Harris*

As I write this, many other stories of my time as a fireman come to mind: the varying routes, the different drivers, the changing experiences, the different engines I worked on. Looking back, I was fortunate to fire the last of the 'Nelsons'. These were on the up or down mail from or to Basingstoke. To me they were tough on the fireman, mainly due to the long firebox. At that time all our engines seemed to be well maintained and I do not recall ever failing on the road. True, we might sometimes be a bit short of steam when on the up road between Winchester and Micheldever, but then it was a simple case of attracting the attention of the signalman and he would route us into the loop. It happened to everyone at some stage, but somehow the shed would find out and there would invariably be ribald comments for a while afterwards.

I liked the Bulleids. I have mentioned No 34105 in original condition on the 'Pines', but I was lucky enough also to work rebuilt No 34009 *Lyme Regis* in ex-works condition between Fratton and Southampton Central via Netley when in charge of a through service from Brighton to Plymouth. As regards the tank engines, the 'M7s' were well-liked by all, and the Standard classes were easy to work on, even if a they could give a harsh ride; in fact, the only type I really did not like was the 'USA' Class, but then I don't think many did.

I could never have imagined at the tender age of six that all of this would have opened up to me, but then neither could I have imagined some of the unusual booking-on times associated with railway work – 1.05am, 3.42pm, 11.59pm – never a straightforward 9.00am start with a 5.00pm finish.

I mentioned before about the promotion structure: engine cleaner, passed cleaner, fireman, passed fireman, driver. I have been in the situation where my driver was a passed fireman and I was just a passed cleaner, both of us thus stepping up one grade – unusual but still quite legitimate.

When I look back, the structure and operation of the engine shed was very complex. Neither can one ignore the fact that a steam shed is totally different from a diesel depot. The Eastleigh diesel depot, built in the late 1950s to service the arrival of the first multiple unit sets, was situated a little further along Campbell Road and compared with the steam shed was relatively clean. Obviously there was no coal, but it did come with numerous barrels of oil and other lubricants scattered around. Not quite clinically clean, but certainly not far off.

Meanwhile, back at the steam shed and housed within the huge office building with the water tank on the top were two floors of offices, including that of the Shed Master. On the ground floor were toilets, male only, the 'signing-on' office, a room full of duty rosters – duty numbers near which would be a list of which engine went with which duty – and the cabin for the drivers and firemen to sit in while awaiting their next turn. This is where the booked spare crews also waited and where I was sitting on the day I was sent to Bournemouth. Being called to take up a spare duty would also depend on how

A steam shed in decline: this is the rear of Eastleigh on 8 August 1966. Two engines are present, Class 4 tank No 80139 and an unidentified '75xxx' – not helped by having lost its front numberplate. Repairs both to engines and infrastructure were now down to minimal level; for example, the missing corrugated sheeting on the shed would never be replaced. *Tony Harris*

Towards the end, the men would pick their way past lines now cold and rusting where once there had been life. Here two 'Moguls', Nos 31408 and 31639, await their fate at the rear of the shed on 8 August 1966.

long it had been since you had actually booked on. For example, if you had already been waiting for 4 hours 'spare', and the turn that needed to be covered meant you would likely be away for 6 hours, it would instead be given to a crew who had only recently arrived.

At Eastleigh we had a turntable that was well balanced and a man whose sole duty was to look after it. As a result it moved easily, unlike the one at Southampton Terminus, which needed a considerable amount of physical 'push', notwithstanding the low gearing the operating handles were supposed to achieve. Even so, at Eastleigh the shed turntable was not large enough for the biggest engines, the 'Pacifics' and 9Fs, so these were instead sent to turn on the triangle at the back of the shed. Beyond the far end was simply rough countryside, while to the right was the Airport and to the left the back end of the works. Speaking of the triangle, I recall when one particular engine cleaner thought he would have a go at driving (no, it was not Dopey, mentioned last time – he had left by now). Up he climbed on to the footplate and opened the regulator to make the engine move, but then panicked as he could not close it – perhaps the water was too high in the boiler. Whatever, he jumped off the moving engine. Fortunately all the points were set towards the triangle, but at the far end was a buffer stop, albeit perhaps not of the conventional type as might be imagined. Instead it was a massive block of solid concrete, its purpose being to stop a recalcitrant engine heading its way from whatever cause.

Now it would be put to the test – concrete versus steam... The concrete won, the engine suffering damaged buffers, and the culprit (not the engine) was reprimanded.

Time moved on and together with countless others I endured my share of preparation and disposal, cleaning out fireboxes and smokeboxes, dodging red-hot cylinders and hot ash as best I could.

Come 1966, I was 20 years old and the rundown of steam was obvious. The writing was 'on the wall' and invariably the subject of many crews' conversations concerned the uncertainty for the future with the increased arrival of diesel engines and work towards electrification. To go or to stay was what the men were asking, especially the firemen, as we could see the future for a second-man was not certain in the longer term.

We had the 'D65xx' breed at Eastleigh, later known as Class 33, and one of my first turns on a diesel was when I was second-man on one hauling 'dead' No 30850 *Lord Nelson* as

Memories of busier times: this is one of Stephen Townroe's views of the rear of Eastleigh shed during the unfortunate ASLEF strike of 1955. The term 'unfortunate' is used deliberately, as the outcome of the stoppage was hardly the result the footplate crews had been after, while during the strike many previously loyal rail users, both passenger and freight, were forced to take recourse in alternative available road transport – and never returned.

far as Didcot. It did appear strange to be sitting alongside the driver, but not doing a lot. The driver's job had also changed, of course. He could now come to work in a white shirt and tie if he wanted. No dirty coal and none of the associated aspects of the steam engine – a new era was here, and there was even talk of issuing drivers with briefcases. What for was not specified. It was all very simple stuff on a diesel: insert the master key, move a lever or two and press a button.

All the diesel engine required to start was – a key. At the end of the shift, turn off the key – simple. With fewer steam engines, fewer firemen, me included, were required.

Things changed soon after this, and probably due to a surplus of firemen I was given a temporary job in the neighbouring works. I was working in a very large hut, which was also extremely warm, making up oil wicks, that consumable but essential device on a steam engine that allowed the oil to get to the relevant bearing. The next thing I knew I was simply overcome by the heat. I had tests to check my health, which previously had been good, but even one such episode was not good news as it might happen again on a hot footplate. The result was that I was sidelined and taken off the footplate for a few weeks, being moved to the checking-in office.

Now I was with some of the men mentioned right at the start of this narrative: Percy Eames, Frank Tarrant, Sam Noyce (known as 'Noisy Noyce') and Percy Black. Percy Black used to cover 'Queenie', the engine cleaning supervisor, whenever he was off work. When Percy covered, he could often be found in the checking-in office, leaving the engine cleaners to themselves. Sam was called 'Noisy' because he used to get very excited when he spoke and increased the volume of his voice. Despite the change I was still working the various shifts and would often go out with either Frank or Sam in the shed's sliding-door Commer van to deliver a 'call-out' notice. Years ago this would have been done by a 'call boy', usually the junior cleaner, who would make his way around the various crews' homes delivering a note to tell them what time their next turn was – any time within the next 18 hours. The paper form was about 6 inches square and could easily be lost or misplaced, should the recipient wish it so ... all very different from being on the footplate and satisfying my dream job.

It was a hard decision, but one that had to be made, and in late 1966 I left the railway, not long before the end of Southern steam, which occurred in the summer of 1967. There was now a new direction, a career in the Post Office, where I remained for 35 years – good times, but never the same as my days as Eastleigh or, of course, the highlight of that one all-too-brief trip on No 34105.

Southern Civil Engineering

Some little time ago, Peter Tatlow (he of 'Railway Breakdown Cranes' fame) allowed us to have copies of an album of images of which he had once temporarily been custodian, detailing some of the civil engineering operations of the SR in the inter-war period. Other than the occasional word identifying some, but not all, of the locations, there were no captions, but even so they provide for a most interesting perspective on some of the work undertaken by the SR in the period, both new work and repairs/maintenance.

These views show the construction and completion of the new electric car sheds at Orpington at varying dates in the spring and early summer of 1925. It was built on the site of four existing sidings, and was in connection with the electrification of the Charing Cross to Orpington electric service, which commenced in February 1926. In one of the views a steam engine is seen, implying that much of the work was either undertaken by or with the assistance of railway resources. Indeed, the SR, like the other railway companies, had the facility to undertake much major civil engineering work itself. Prior to the start of the electric service, Orpington had boasted a small two-road engine shed and turntable, but these were taken out of use with the introduction of the electric service, the turntable being removed and the former engine shed given over to a new use as a permanent way depot. Interestingly, access to the new electric sheds was via a shunt move rather than direct from the running lines.

A further image, regretfully unsuitable for publication, shows a line of brand-new 'SUB' sets in the depot; it is dated 14 June 1926, indicating that early deliveries had taken place and that the shed itself was also complete by this time. This basic design of what was official designated a 'cleaning shed' was commonplace at numerous locations on the SR. Several also survive into the 21st century, albeit with replacement external cladding.

Another 'cleaning shed' under construction, this time the larger example at Addiscombe Road, recorded in April 1925. Of interest here is the 'GN' (Great Northern) open wagon, of the 'common-user' type, so likely purloined for general use by the SR – there is, of course, always the possibility that it had actually arrived with materials from that company's lines. Other analogous views depict wagons representing the MR, LMS and SECR in similar poses.

We could not resist including this second view of the same location, this time two months later in June 1925. Just look at the workers perched on the girders above and the men underneath. Comparisons with modern-day safety have been regularly made both in 'SW' and elsewhere, but it does highlight the dangers faced by the average worker going about his daily tasks during this period.

Concluding the car shed sequence, we *think* the last three of these are of Slade Green and its associated repair shop, all taken around September 1925. (Some of the images are annotated with date and location, others require a guessing game.) The views show the repair shop and some brand-new units, hopefully not in need of repairs yet! The electric depot here was converted from the former steam shed, although likely it was just the site that was used rather than the actual steam shed structure. The buildings are also to a different design from that previously seen.

A small but essential component of the expansion of the electrified network was the provision of impedance bonds at places where insulated fishplates were used to commence or end track circuits. As will be known, the SR third-rail network used a third rail for the live pick-up with the return passing via the running rail. When an insulated rail joint was reached, this would impede the return path so the impedance bond, an iron-core coil of low resistance and relatively high reactance, was used to provide a continuous path around the joint for the return propulsion current. We are not given the location.

This view shows the sub-station at Lewisham on 30 August 1925, noted as recorded to show the numerous cable outlet runs.

This extended platform and platform wall were photographed at Honor Oak Park on 30 August 1925. Note the mechanical-arm ground signal controlling the exit from the siding. The view is looking towards Nunhead.

This rebuilt overbridge is at Sundridge Park, between Grove Park and Bromley North, also photographed on 30 August 1925.

These two views of Herne Hill station in the course of rebuilding were taken in June and August 1925 respectively.

New bridges and a viaduct at Lewisham, seen on 30 May 1929.

This is Tattenham Corner on the first day of the new electric service, 25 March 1928. Some clearing-up still remains to be done, but it is obvious that steam will be no more as the bags have been removed from the water columns. Note also the concrete-post signals. What are those two coaches in the background?

Part of the complex tangle of lines sometimes known as the Selhurst triangle. We are looking north east towards Norwood Junction along the East Croydon Local Spur. Visible behind the bridge is the tall Norwood Fork Junction signal box of 1902 which lasted until the resignalling of the area in 1954. On the left is part of the Power Station Siding with the structure itself (which looks new) prominent and which was evidently the subject of the photograph. With thanks to John Minnis for the location information.

There will be a few more from the same source in a later edition, but in the meanwhile and continuing on the theme of electrification...

The EPB Story Part 7
1957 and 1960 Stock
David Monk-Steel

(Previous instalments in this series appeared in issues 20, 24, 25, 26, 37, and 38.)

With the impending electrification of the lines to the Kent Coast, new outer-suburban and express stock were ordered. The existing 2-HAP, 4-BEP and 4-CEP designs were selected for this, but the control and electrical equipment was updated to the latest specification, although compatibility with earlier rolling stock was maintained.

The 1957 stock introduced camshaft control, instead of the electro-pneumatic interlock-operated switch control of the 1951 stock, consisting of oil/electro-pneumatic vane actuators operated by the master controller driving the camshaft, to open and close resistance and weak field contacts of the power circuits in the correct sequence. Another change, on the four-car units of 1957 stock, was a single motor generator and a battery provided on only one of the motor coaches within a set. This modification was undertaken because of proven reliability of the equipment on previous stock. The 1957-type stock was not fitted with main power switches, therefore the current was fed direct from the power junction box to the equipment fuse. On the 1957 stock, the power circuit fuses were all of shoe fuse pattern and fitted the standard type of shoe fuse box. In the driver's cab the 'fuse' cupboard also now contained 70-volt miniature circuit breakers instead of replaceable fuses.

A feature of the 1957 stock brought about by the electrification to Folkestone Harbour was the inclusion of a 'series switch' in the cab. This prevented the control equipment 'notching up' to parallel position while climbing the 1 in 30 incline, and was to protect the resistances from overheating. The 1951 stock did not have this feature and should not have been attached as the leading vehicles when departing from Folkestone Harbour (in practice the 1951 stock rarely found its way to this part of the system).

The end of steam on the South Eastern: SECR 'L' No 31765, likely working one of its last duties on the South Eastern lines, heads a Dover-line train consisting of all-BR Mark 1 stock in carmine and cream livery. The photographer, P. Ransome Wallis, unfortunately does not identify the exact location, but he does make mention of the sign to the right, adding the comment, 'And some would say not before time,' perhaps implying that passengers were somewhat disillusioned with the steam service that then existed. Mention of the sign itself, note the word 'Southern' at the top instead of 'Southern Region', which might have been expected – a case perhaps of company loyalty still remaining strong? No 31765 was subsequently transferred to the Western Section at Nine Elms but did not last long there, being withdrawn in February 1961.

The new carriages were built using the same patterns and jigs as Mark 1 carriages. The 2-HAPs incorporated standard suburban structural components, with a door to each compartment flanked by a quarter-light. The Driving Trailer Composite incorporated a side corridor to the 1st Class section, giving sole access to a lavatory compartment at the centre of the carriage. This toilet compartment occupied half the width of the vehicle, a 2nd Class lavatory occupying the other half. The 2nd Class section was arranged in the standard open saloon style with a central gangway. The Driving Motor Brake Second vehicle was similar to the 2-EPB DMBS. Externally the stock was also 'tidied up' when compared to the earlier 1951 stock. The roof conduits typical of the latter (and the previous SR stock) were not perpetuated, and all wiring ran through the train in concealed conduits. The stock was constructed at Eastleigh and delivered in three batches.

1957 Phase 1 stock

The first batch was intended for Phase 1 of the Kent Coast electrification scheme from Gillingham to Sheerness, Ramsgate and Dover Marine, which was completed in 1959.

For the stopping services, some more 2-HAP units were supplied. This batch, to the 1957 design, was numbered 6043 to 6105 and introduced between November 1958 and September 1959. The internal layout was identical to the previous batch with a Driving Motor Brake Second and a Driving Trailer Lavatory Composite. The headcode panel was still the taller variety found on the 1951 stock. At first the larger numeral blinds were employed, but by the time Phase 2 was commissioned more compact numerals were being used and the aperture was masked to suit.

For the express services Eastleigh turned out more four-car sets similar in layout to the six-car units introduced in 1956. The 4-BEP units were Nos 7003 to 7012 with a buffet car and Corridor Composite Trailers, with 4-CEP units Nos 7105 to 7153 having a Corridor Second instead of the buffet. These sets appeared between August 1958 and August 1959. The English Electric 507-type traction motors were identical to earlier stock, giving a level balancing speed of 72mph.

Originally too the Phase 1 batch of 1957 4-CEP/4-BEP units had double-glazing to the large windows, but there were problems with the seal between the panes and many were replaced with single-glazed units.

Like the original 1951 stock, the 1957 Phase 1 stock vehicles were carried on Mark 3 or Mark 4 bogies, a development of the steam-hauled-stock Mark 1 type. These were similar to those fitted to the Hastings DEMUs with lateral shock absorbers, shear-type rubber auxiliary springs and rubber-bonded spherical bearings for the bolster swing hangers. In practice they did not ride well at speed and experiments were carried out on 1951 set No 7101 using the much more expensive and heavier 'Commonwealth' bogie, but with considerable success. The buffet cars of the 1957 Phase 1 4-BEPs eventually received Commonwealth bogies, but the rest of the Phase 1 stock retained its original bogies with some suspension modifications to try and overcome the poor ride quality. By April 1960 2-HAP No 6074 had Commonwealth trailer bogies, as did the buffet car of set No 7010.

Unlike the 1956-built 4-CEP units, the interior was finished with plastic laminate, and the windows were framed in wood, sycamore or ash. In the Driving Motor Second Brakes, a matt steel-blue plastic finish was employed between and beneath the

A 12-car train headed by 4-CEP No 7123 is seen during a test run at Wallington on 15 January 1959. Notice the air whistle above the driver's window, and the whole train painted in the then standard EMU green livery. *J. L. Smith*

An official view of one of the new trains. Again the air whistle is visible, as well as the guard's periscope.

windows with a gloss black panel backing beneath the window to accept the ash trays and table mounting. The ends of the saloons were finished in gloss white plastic, and the ceilings were light grey matt. In the Trailer Corridor Second compartments, below and alongside the windows was in matt red plastic, with a black panel beneath the window. Matt green plastic was used in the Trailer Composite. Ceilings were also finished in light grey matt and the ends of the saloons were finished in gloss white plastic.

The new Phase 1 trains came into service in June 1959, replacing steam traction on the routes from Victoria, Cannon Street and Charing Cross to Ramsgate, Dover Marine and Sheerness-on-Sea via Chatham.

The hourly express services were formed of two 4-CEP units flanking a 4-BEP. On the down journey the train split into two portions at Gillingham, with the leading 4-CEP together with the 4-BEP running non-stop to Whitstable, then all stations from Herne Bay to Ramsgate, while the rear 4-CEP called at all principal stations to Dover Marine. The up journey operated a similar pattern in reverse. An hourly semi-fast service between Victoria and Sheerness was formed of 2-HAP units in various combinations depending upon the time of the day, some services detaching a Maidstone East portion at Swanley. An hourly Charing Cross to Ramsgate service was also formed of 2-HAP units running semi-fast over the North Kent, then calling at all stations from Strood to Ramsgate. An hourly stopping service from Sheerness to Dover Priory formed of 2-HAP stock was also introduced, as well as an hourly Sheerness to Sittingbourne local service.

There were also extra Kent Coast business trains morning and evening to and from Cannon Street or Victoria, mainly formed of 4-CEP/4-BEP/4-CEP, and a service formed of 2-HAP stock from Sheerness to Cannon Street in the morning and back again at night.

Prior to their introduction, some of the new sets were stored between Horsted Keynes and Ardingly on the down line, and the up line was used temporarily for bi-directional working between the two stations mentioned. Temporary electric token working was installed to provide for safe operation.

Trials of these new trains were carried out on the Brighton main line, and a number of experiments were undertaken. In early 1960 unit No 7133 was given a yellow band painted above the 1st Class compartments of the composite carriage, and was provided with smaller headcode numerals than previously. In April that year further units appeared with the yellow 1st Class indicator line at cantrail level, and 4-BEP units Nos 7010 and 7012 also had a red line below the cantrail for the entire length of the catering vehicle. This arrangement eventually became a standard marking for 1st Class and restaurant facilities.

1957 Phase 2 Stock

Phase 2 of the Kent Coast scheme in 1961 saw the routes via Tonbridge and Ashford electrified, and further 2-HAP, 4-BEP and 4-CEP sets were constructed to replace the steam trains. Electrically they were the same as the Phase 1 sets, but mechanically and structurally these new units incorporated improvements compared to the Phase 1 rolling stock, not least being fitted with Commonwealth bogies to replace the Mark 1-derived bogies fitted to the earlier stock in an attempt to improve the riding qualities. There had been numerous complaints about the riding of the first Phase 1 units; as a consequence tests had been carried out and it was decided that the Commonwealth-type cast steel bogie was a much better option even at the disadvantage of an increase in the weight of the train.

Motor bogies for Phase 2 stock were of the 'Mark 3B' type, which again incorporated improvements over the Mark 1 motor bogies of earlier Southern Region stock. There were other differences as well as changes to fittings. As examples, the water tanks for the lavatories were mounted under the floor with a pressure feed. Litter bins were fitted to the trailing ends of the motor coaches, and also in the corridor at the non-lavatory end of the TSK and the 2nd Class end of the TCK. Some motor coaches had a 'swinging' door in the partition separating the smoking and non-smoking areas.

Electric traction was also now being provided for the prestige 'Golden Arrow'. An unidentified Class 71 (E50xx series) locomotive passes Otford with the service, diverted due to engineering work between Orpington and Sevenoaks. What had also once been an all-Pullman service now has the first few vehicles as ordinary stock. *G. G. Akhurst*

During the transition from steam, No D5010 stands at Ashford with the 12.28pm Maidstone East to Margate service on 19 May 1959, made up solely of Bulleid stock. The SR had 15 of these engines as a temporary measure pending full electrification in Kent. Unfortunately as supplied they were considered too heavy for the SR and were required to have their steam heat boilers removed before being accepted. Later, as Class 24, all were moved to the LMR, ER and ScR. *D. C. Ovenden*

A brace of the type, Nos D5009 leading D5011, pass Sandling with a Victoria to Folkestone boat train. *Derek Cross*

The new Phase 2 2-HAP, 4-CEP and 4-BEP units had the smaller roller blind numerals from the outset, although the headcode panel remained the same size as previous stock but the apertures were masked to accommodate the smaller numerals.

Set numbers for the new units were 7154 to 7202, with Driving Motor Brake Second coaches allocated in odd and even pairs in the series S61694 to S61791 in order, Trailer Corridor Seconds S70503 to S70551, and Trailer Corridor Composites S70552 to S70600, also allocated in numerical order. The 4-BEP units, Nos 7013 to 7022, were made up from Driving Motor Brake Second saloon coaches S61792 to S61811, Trailer Corridor Composites S70601 to S70610, and buffet cars S69012 to S69021. Two further units, Nos 7203 and 7204, were added in 1961. 2-HAP sets were made up as Nos 6106 to 6046, Driving Motor Brake Seconds S61648 to S61688 attached to Driving Trailer Lavatory Composites S75700 to S75740.

Services between Dover and Ramsgate via Minster were electrically operated from 2 January 1961, although initially running under steam timings. The line from Sevenoaks to Folkestone with the branch to Maidstone West from Paddock Wood was energised in May 1961 and full public electrically worked services commenced on 12 June. Even so there was still some work to complete, and the Maidstone East to Minster via Ashford portion of the route was still worked by locomotive-hauled trains for the time being, final electrification being completed on 9 October.

To try and reduce the effect of rainwater splashing passengers, a rectangular-section vertical gutter was added to the sides of certain vehicles about 6 inches from each of the ends. 4-CEP No 7190 was first noted with this modification early in 1961. In late 1961 4-CEP No 7115 was experimentally fitted with two motor bogies under one motor coach and two trailer bogies under the other for high-speed tests.

As a trial, 4-CEP No 7146 and Hastings DEMU No 1018 were given a yellow warning panel painted on each end in early 1962. This panel was vertical in shape and of a similar size to a gangway door. At the same time 4-SUB No 4378 and 4-EPB No 5048 were given a panel beneath the cab windows. The latter arrangement was adopted as standard from January 1964. On two-coach units, an inverted black triangle was to be applied to the end where the luggage van was situated; this was to alert staff that the other end of the unit (when running singly) did not have a luggage van. In late 1961 the interior of the driving cabs of 2-HAPs Nos 6135 and 6138 were also painted white instead of the usual light green.

1957 Suburban stock

In 1960 a series of 4-EPB stock of BR standard design was introduced to eliminate the last of the pre-war augmented 3-SUB sets. The first two sets, Nos 5301 and 5302, consisted of a pair of BR-type 1957 Driving Motor Brake Seconds with two spare SR Bulleid-type Trailer Second saloons between. The DMBSs had two four-bay saloons separated from each other by a partition, giving a seating capacity of 84. The Bulleid trailers in the first two sets were the standard SR layout with a ten-compartment Trailer Second (TS) and a ten-bay Trailer Second Saloon (TSO). It is thought that these units were authorised as replacements for accident damage to earlier 4-EPB stock.

New-build Suburban stock under construction at Eastleigh on 17 February 1956.

Looking a bit travel-stained, 4-CEP No 7009 is seen at Whitstable. The unit retains its air whistle and has the side destination brackets in use. *P. J. Sharpe*

The next 54 sets had new-build trailers to BR design. These Trailer Second vehicles were originally of the semi-saloon layout, half of the seating being compartments, the other half having a central passage between the seats. They seated 112 persons in a saloon of five bays and in five compartments. In service the compartment ends of the trailer cars were usually marshalled adjacent to each other. The trailer bogies were to a Mark 3 design.

The motor coaches of Nos 5301 and 5302 and all of those numbered 5303 to 5356 were 1957 stock. Driving Motor Brake Seconds S61625 and S61626 in No 5301 were fitted with air whistles, but the motor coaches of No 5302 upwards were fitted with air horns; on unit Nos 5303 to 5315 and 5317 the horns were embedded in the cab front just over the windows, but for the rest they were attached to the roof above the driving cab windows facing forward. It is believed that complaints from drivers initiated this change. Motor coaches of Nos 5303 to 5356 were numbered S61516 to S61623, and the trailers were S70375 to 70482.

Set No 5302 was formed from S61627 and S61872. This unit was introduced considerably later than No 5301. Its trailer cars were S15079S (ex S10195S) and S15121S.

The headcode roller blinds of this batch retained the taller style for the present and received these from express stock that was being fitted with the smaller pattern from 1960 onwards.

Notwithstanding the bogie changes compared with earlier sets, the riding of these units continued to give concern in late 1961 and early 1962, especially Nos 5345 to 5356, and various modifications were tried by Eastleigh Works. Trailer S70479 in No 5355 was fitted with bogie-mounted brake cylinders as a trial. Nos 5341, 5344 and 5355 were then fitted with three-position brake valves in 1963.

Additional sets, Nos 5357 to 5370 (sometimes considered as a sub-group of the '1960 stock'), were built at Eastleigh from 1962; their motor coaches were S61989 to S62016, attached to trailers S70667 to S70694. These '1960 stock' sets incorporated a number of detailed differences from the earlier batch, most noticeably in the route indicator box, which was reduced in height to more closely accommodate the smaller number blinds; they also had BR3C trailer bogies.

No 5800, the solitary 1957 2-EPB

Introduced in January 1960 as a replacement for accident-damaged stock, set No 5800 was the solitary example of a 1957-type 2-EPB. It does not appear to have lasted very long and was disbanded, the individual carriages being used to replace accident-damaged vehicles in other sets. Motor Brake Second semi-saloon S61624 was originally fitted with an air whistle. The Driving Trailer Second semi-saloon was S75636, and was equipped with BR4 bogies in the summer of 1962 for testing purposes. For completeness, vehicle S61624 was substituted for one of the motor coaches of set No 5352 in early 1964. This set had run away from Bromley North on the afternoon of 29 October 1962, resulting in a collision with a bridge pillar at Grove Park and serious damage to vehicles S61614 and S70473. S75636 was stored and later ended up in No 5710.

MLV S68003 runs solo up from Dover, passing Kearnsey on 16 August 1981.

The Motor Luggage Vans

Specifically constructed to handle the extra baggage associated with travellers using the short sea route between Dover, Folkestone and Newhaven and the French and Belgian ports, the Southern Region ordered ten self-propelled luggage vans that could operate in multiple with the new express stock.

The North Eastern Region had already taken delivery of one similar van (E68000) for use on the South Shields third-rail section, and it was also similar in layout to a locomotive-hauled BG Luggage Brake Van, but with BR EPB-style driving cabs at either end and mounted on a 63ft 5in underframe. Introduced in 1955 at the same time as a fleet of 15 2-EPB-type sets for this section, the NER vehicle had 1951-type control equipment, and featured the exposed conduits attached to the roof. Vacuum brake and air/electro-pneumatic brakes were fitted, and there were four 250hp traction motors so that the van could be used as a locomotive in the third-rail area.

The 10 new Southern Region vehicles were 1957-type stock and had a different layout from the North Eastern van in order to incorporate a bank of lead-acid batteries at the No 1 end; these were provided to enable the vehicles to work away from the third rail singly or in pairs to access the non-electrified portion of the quays at Dover and Folkestone, taking the luggage closer to the ship and so reducing the need for handling. This had the additional advantage of allowing them to work into other non-electrified sidings and to attach non-passenger coaching stock and freight vehicles as necessary. Still 63ft 5in long over the headstocks, they had three pairs of doors on each side, giving access to the luggage space, and a guard's compartment behind the No 1 end driver's cab. There were no gangway connections to the rest of the train, and when working on boat trains the luggage compartment had to be sealed under Customs supervision.

Unlike in the earlier Tyneside van, the SR MLVs had only two 250hp motors, but they were permitted to act as a locomotive hauling 100 tons while drawing current from the third rail, or 50 tons while working on battery power. The batteries were recharged via a motor generator whenever the vehicle was standing with shoes in contact with an energised

A 4-CEP Trailer Composite. *P. J. Sharpe*

2-HAP No 6066, trailing another similar unit, leaves Canterbury for Dover. The use of the oil tail lamp will be noted. *P. J. Sharpe*

third rail. The SR vans were dual-braked and incorporated a proportional valve to enable the vacuum brake to be controlled from a leading EMU if operating in multiple. The pick-up shoes retracted pneumatically when battery power was selected. Two vehicles were delivered during Phase 1 in 1959, the following eight appearing in time to work on the Phase 2 boat trains. They tended to stay on the Eastern Section, but at Christmas it was not totally unusual to see an MLV with one or two SR four-wheel PL vans in tow between London and Redhill.

Numbers were S68001 to S68002 introduced in April 1959, and S68003 to S68006 introduced between December 1960 and January 1961; S68007 to S68009 appeared in February, and S68010 in March.

1957 Express stock, final batches

Seven further 4-CEP units were constructed at Eastleigh in late 1962/early 1963 for the Portsmouth line. The sets were numbered 7205 to 7211; the DMBSOs were S61948 to S61961, the TCKs S70653 to S70659, and the TSKs S70660 to S70666.

A further batch of 2-HAP stock was also introduced for use on the South Western Division, Nos 6147 to 6173 (DMBS S61962 to S61988 and DTCL S75995 to S76021). The last two, Nos 6172 and 6173, were fitted with fluorescent lights. These units and the last batch of BR standard 4-EPBs featured a revised arrangement of rain gutters, with an additional high-level gutter and vertical gutters at the ends of the carriages. All cab ends featured the shorter headcode panel. These 4-CEP units had internal illuminated 'toilet engaged' signs.

Bogies on these new units were the Commonwealth type except for the motor bogies, and the shoe beam bogies on the 2-HAP DTCL, which were Mark 4 (a development of the Mark 1 and improved Mark 3/3B/3C, identifiable by a vertical damper midway along the bogie frame).

Addenda to previous chapters

2-EPB No 5756 was tested with disc brakes in April 1960 on the South London services. These were removed early in 1964 and the unit reverted to normal.

1951-type 4-CEP No 7102 was fitted with disc brakes and BR Mark 4 bogies in November 1961. 4-BEP No 7001 was also so fitted.

Fifteen units of 1951-type 2-EPB-style stock were delivered to the North Eastern Region from Eastleigh in 1955. Similar in most respects to Southern Region 2-EPBs, when the NER de-electrified the South Shields line on 7 January 1963 the redundant sets were earmarked to return south. The original coach numbers were E65311 to E65325 (DMBS) and E77100 to E77114 (DTC), but unlike the Southern the North Eastern Region did not employ set numbers. The principal differences included the route indicator, which as specified for the NER and consisted of an array of five lights in 'playing card' pattern where the SR headcode blind should have been, and with a narrow destination roller blind above. Also the DMBS only had seven seating bays instead of the Southern's eight, allowing a larger luggage van. This was useful to accommodate the high number of children's perambulators that was a feature of seaside days out from Tyneside to the coast! Also the Driving Trailer had a 1st Class-appointed compartment located centrally. However, the overall dimensions were the same as the SR 2-EPB, so that on transfer the seat trim was changed to 2nd Class material, although the double luggage racks were retained. On arrival on the Southern those 'in the know' would seek out this compartment, because the original 1st Class cushions were still there concealed beneath the mundane upholstery.

One modification that would not be obvious was the realignment of the shoe gear, moved 1½ inches outwards to ensure compatibility with the SR conductor rails. Once Eastleigh had 'Southernised' them, these sets were given 'S' prefixes to the coach numbers and were given set numbers 5781 to 5795. The headcode display was also altered to show the now standard SR-pattern small roller blinds, and as with 4-EPBs Nos 5357 to 5370 these were provided with the shorter panel. The seven-compartment arrangement of the DMBS was retained. The units entered service on the SR from August 1963 onwards.

Buffet Car S69000 was experimentally fitted with B4-type air-spring bogies in 1963, but these were later replaced with Commonwealth bogies in the spring of 1964.

Although non-EPB stock had been spasmodically retro-fitted with air horns in place of the air whistle since 1960, instructions were issued that from early 1964 all stock, including EPB, was to be so fitted when passing through the works. Newly built stock had, however, been equipped with air horns since 1960.

The interior of a facelifted BEP buffet car following attention at (of all places) Swindon in 1983. By now designated Class 410 by BR, the '4-CEP' family were the longest-lasting EMU sets based on the Mark 1 carriage design and had a maximum lifespan of 49 years.

Kingston Wharf
The French connection
Jeffrey Grayer

Following the article in SW41 on the role of Littlehampton in the cross-Channel steamer trade, Jeffery Grayer takes a look at the brief heyday of Kingston Wharf along the Sussex coast at Shoreham Harbour, the earliest of the LBSCR's packet ports, together with its long association with Wainwright's diminutive 'P' Class tanks.

John Marius Wilson's *Imperial Gazetteer of England and Wales*, published in the early 1870s, described Kingston-by-Sea thus:

'A parish in Steyning district, Sussex; on the South Coast railway, and at the mouth of Shoreham harbour, one mile east of Shoreham. It has a station on the railway, and a wharf on the harbour. The manor, with Kingston House, belongs to W. P. Gorringe, Esq. Two corn warehouses, large malting houses, railway coke ovens, a ship building yard, bonding warehouses, ponds and quays are here; and a large traffic goes on between the railway station and the harbour.'

Travelling on the top deck of a Southdown double-decker on the A259 coast road from Hove to Shoreham-by-Sea in the late 1950s, one could often obtain a glimpse of a plume of smoke by looking out on the seaward side of the bus as it climbed the slopes of Lower Road at Kingston. The smoke invariably belonged to one of Harry Wainwright's 'P' Class 0-6-0 tank engines designed for the SECR way back in 1910 and to be found eking out its last days shunting wagons on the wharf.

'P' No 31556 is seen in June 1957 at Kingston Wharf. The ship alongside is the *Melissa M*, **a general cargo vessel built in 1956 with a gross tonnage of 994. It carried this name until 1977, when it became the** *Panormitis*. *S. C. Townroe, Colour-Rail*

Quite why there was a wharf here and why these locomotives should be in use is a story of ambitious plans and failed hopes both on the high seas and on the rails.

Back in the 18th century packet boats had begun sailing from Kingston harbour to Dieppe, and by 1788 a regular service was in operation, even though the harbour itself was far from ideal. This was due mainly to the fact that the nearby River Adur had a tendency to build up a sand bar where it met the sea, moving its mouth progressively eastwards. Efforts to keep the harbour mouth clear were not entirely successful until 1817-21 when the present entrance to the harbour was constructed

Our story begins in 1838 when a wharf was constructed at Kingston in Shoreham Harbour at the mouth of the River Adur primarily as a landing place for building materials for the firm of Hayle & Wythes. This firm was the contractor for the Shoreham section of the London & Brighton Railway (L&BR), precursor of the LBSCR, the 'West Coast Line' from Brighton. When the line was opened in May 1840, a year before rails were to reach the premier Sussex resort from the capital, the railway company assumed ownership of the wharf. This decision was prompted by two main considerations. One was the import of coal and the local conversion there of coal into coke, which was possible in the coke ovens built in an area behind the wharf. This in turn enabled the bulk of the coke, which was used in the railway company's locomotives at that time, to be supplied more cheaply and to a higher grade than previous local coal merchants could achieve. Of greater significance, however, was the opportunity that the wharf gave, and for the L&BR to announce that 'The quickest route to Paris is by the railway to Shoreham and thence by packet to Dieppe'. For a number of years previously a service of cross-Channel packets had operated from Shoreham and Brighton to Dieppe and Le Havre, but it was only now that rail with connections to the capital gave the whole enterprise a new significance. The establishment of a permanent entrance to Shoreham Harbour was followed in 1830 by completion of a new Custom House.

On the completion of the Brighton-Shoreham line, a station was opened at Kingston enabling rail passengers to take ship from the nearby wharf on board the PS *Magnate*, one of the vessels of the General Steam Navigation Company (GSNC), which sailed to Dieppe on Mondays, Wednesdays, Thursdays and Saturdays, and to Le Havre on Tuesdays and Fridays. In 1844 the GSNC and the L&BR coordinated their timetables and, with two new vessels, the PS *Menai* and PS *Fame*, two weekly return trips were made between Shoreham and Dieppe on Wednesdays and Saturdays. Passengers arriving at Dieppe were able to take the road coach for Rouen, where the train service of the Paris & Rouen Railway could be used for the onward journey to Paris, the railway not having reached Dieppe at this time.

Although the wharf was connected to the main line, this was only by means of a cable-worked inclined plane and wagon turntables, so passenger coaches were not able to reach the wharf itself. Therefore passengers had to make their own way to and from the wharf either on foot or by using local conveyances. Various locomotives were used to supply steam for working the inclined plane including, in 1878 for example, Craven mixed-traffic 0-4-2 tender engine No 156, which had been built in Brighton in 1862. In 1926 a Stroudley 'E1' 0-6-0T No 136, formerly *Brindisi* and built in 1878, was also used for this purpose for some months.

Initially the Turnpike Trustees had objected to the line to the wharf crossing the main coast road, and it was to be a year after the opening of the Shoreham line that an agreement was reached to lay a crossing over the road. In later years the road was raised to cross the line on a bridge, but at the cost of a height restriction under the bridge that severely limited the classes of locomotive that could use the line.

The Kingston facility really took off when the Brighton-London line opened in 1841, and two years later the L&BR announced that in the event of a late arrival of the packet from Dieppe, thereby missing the 6.30pm train from Brighton, a special through train would be provided from Kingston to London. By 1844 through carriages from the capital to Kingston were provided for 1st Class passengers, although the lower

The Kingston Wharf signal box diagram of about 1920 shows the connections to the wharf from the down siding via wagon turntables and an inclined plane. (Images of the wharf itself have proven elusive, but the reader is referred to *South Coast Railways: Brighton to Chichester* published by Middleton Press.)
Signalling Record Society

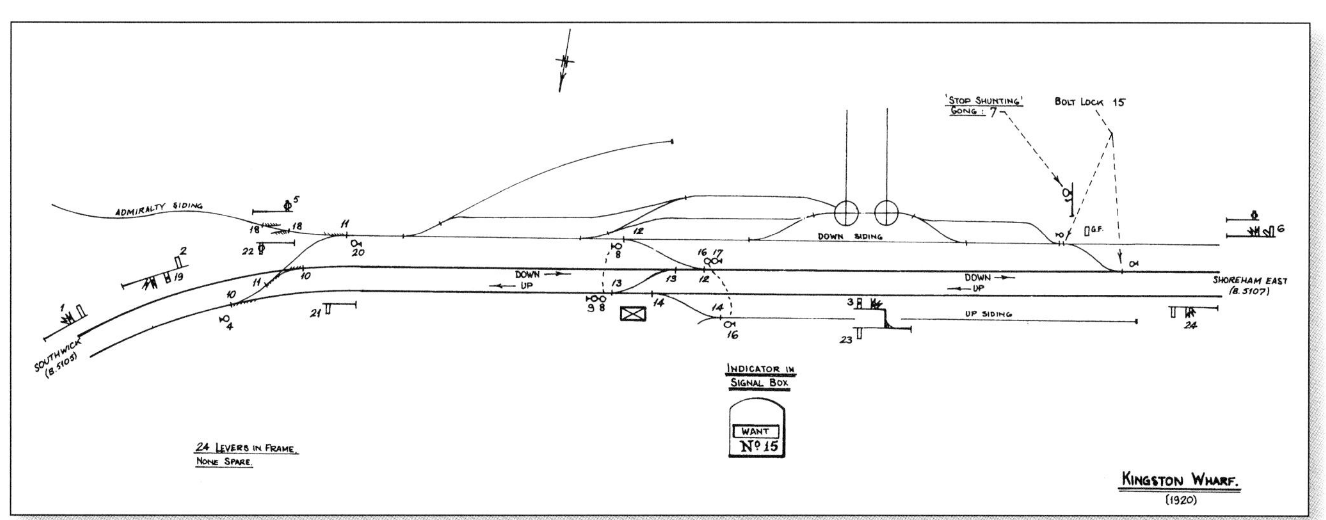

orders had to detrain at Brighton while the stock was shunted from the London to the West Coast platforms at the terminus, this being well before the Cliftonville curve was provided to remove this reversal manoeuvre at Brighton. (For an explanation of this type of working at Brighton, the reader is referred to 'Southern Way Special Issue No 15'.)

Many of the packets from Shoreham sailed via Brighton calling at the Chain Pier, which, opening in 1822, removed the necessity for the perilous transhipment in small boats from the beach to the waiting steamers. However, calls at the Pier were 'weather permitting' and the railway's own advertisements suggested that transfer from rail to ship was made as often at Kingston as at Brighton due to this factor, the railway running connecting trains from Kingston to Brighton in these circumstances.

In addition to cross-Channel passenger traffic, Shoreham Harbour was to handle prodigious quantities of coal, rising from some 21,000 tons in 1838 to 630,000 tons a century later, more than half of the latter total being consumed locally by the gas and electricity works situated on the harbourside.

As previously mentioned, access to the wharf was by no means straightforward. Sidings on the wharf were connected to those on the down side of the main line by inclined planes, passing under the main road, which were at right angles to both sets of sidings and had wagon turntables at each end. Further wagon turntables allowed access to other wharf sidings. Wagons were hauled around the wharf by horse power and ascended the incline attached to chains operated by a stationary engine. Wagons were restricted to a maximum wheelbase of 11ft 9in and the Appendix to the Working Timetable ruled that 'Goods must not be loaded in box wagons exceeding 11 feet in height from rail level', so it was no wonder that the sight of boat trains on the quay was an impossible dream in these circumstances. This situation was not to be addressed for the simple reason that the days of Kingston as a packet station were numbered.

So popular had the service become that a committee was established by the L&BR to examine the possibility of the railway company purchasing its own vessels. The committee duly recommended the formation of a subsidiary, the Brighton & Continental Steam Packet Company, and this was indeed established in 1845, operating its own vessels two years later. The GSNC was worried by this new development and gave notice to the LBSCR, as the L&BR had become after joining with the London & Croydon Railway in July 1846, that joint sailings would cease in November 1846. However, it was decided that in view of the extra hour taken to load and unload passengers at Brighton on the Shoreham-Dieppe route, the underpowered craft available at that time could not make the crossing in one high tide. An alternative option was to use Newhaven Harbour, which would allow the new vessels then being built to make the crossing in less than 5 hours in normal weather conditions. Both Shoreham and Newhaven Harbour Boards were asked what improvements they could make to accommodate railway shipping services. After a long period Shoreham declined to improve its current facilities or to reduce charges, whereas Newhaven, eager to attract the lucrative traffic, promised improvements on both counts.

Thus it was that Newhaven, connected by rail in 1847, became the LBSCR's principal cross-Channel port from August 1845, and the great days of Kingston, which had lasted for just five years, were over. From humble beginnings at a small contractor's wharf in Shoreham Harbour, the ferry services of the LBSCR grew to become the fourth largest railway-owned passenger ferry service in the country. A further blow to Kingston came in 1849 when the LBSCR opened a new coke wharf at Deptford on the Thames, where most of the coal for railway use was now landed. The Kingston coke ovens were demolished in 1890 and two additional sidings laid in their place. Even so, the loss of the passenger ferry and coal trade did not affect Kingston as dramatically as might have been expected, for new firms had moved in, including a malthouse, shipyard and steam sawmill, all making use of the facilities at the wharf. Even fruit and eggs were imported from Normandy. LBSCR packets were also still seen at Kingston, as many were over-wintered at the wharf, where repainting and repairs were still undertaken.

A second, if short-lived, string to Kingston's bow was provided by H. P. Maples, an insurance and shipbroker based in Shoreham, who signed an agreement with the LBSCR in August 1850 to commence a service between Kingston Wharf, Shoreham and the Channel Island of Jersey. This was intended to be a regular service connecting with trains of the LBSCR. Initially it was operated by the *Ladybird*, an iron screw steamer of 353 gross tons built by Denny of Dumbarton and launched early in that same year. A graceful steamer of the time with a fine clipper bow, she could manage a speed of 11 knots. As the advertisement reproduced here indicates, the service was twice weekly and at the time of the announcement was operated by the 'splendid new and fast iron steamship "Brighton"'. In 1851 the Shoreham service was transferred to Newhaven, still operated by Maples, though in close conjunction with the LBSCR.

An 1857 advertisement for the Shoreham-Channel Islands service.

Above: **No 31556 was a regular visitor at both Brighton and Kingston. This was the first of the class to be built at Ashford in 1909 and after service with BR was subsequently saved for preservation. It currently resides on the Kent & East Sussex Railway.**

Right: **Horse shunting at Kingston. The shunter is holding a sprag for moving or chocking wagon wheels.** *Lens of Sutton*

The railway station at Kingston was to become a permanent casualty of the withdrawal of the cross-Channel ferry service, closing on 1 April 1879 due to lack of patronage in spite of a name change to perhaps the more enticing 'Kingston-on-Sea' in 1870. The station house can still be seen today, although of course the platforms have long gone. With only freight traffic to be handled, improvements in rail access to the wharf had to wait until 1938.

In that year the separate basins were infilled with shingle brought from Dungeness to provide a piled straight frontage to the quay. The inclined plane was replaced by a tightly curving locomotive-worked line, descending at a gradient of 1 in 82 with a diamond crossing replacing the wagon turntables. There was restricted access under the A259 road bridge and this, together with the sharply curving dock sidings, required the use of specialist locomotive power. Exit the horse and enter the iron horse in the shape of Wainwright's 'P' Class tanks. Designed by the CME of the SECR to overcome problems with the notoriously unreliable railmotors of the time, the 'P' tanks never really lived up to expectations in that role. Only eight examples were built in 1909-10 and most critics have compared them unfavourably with their near relations, the LSWR 'B4s' and the LBSCR 'Terriers'. Whatever their merits, by the time I came across them they had been relegated to a few duties, their speciality being the lightly laid, sharply curving dock lines of the SR network. By 1959 three had already gone, the remainder being allocated to Dover, Folkestone and Brighton. All were to go by the summer of 1961.

I remember seeing No 31556 at 75A during my periodic weekend visits in 1960/61, and it is from here that some of their last duties were worked. No 31558 had been withdrawn from Folkestone in February 1960 and No 31325 from Brighton in March, both being scrapped at Ashford Works. This left only No 31027 at Dover, No 31323 at Eastleigh, where it occasionally deputised for the Winchester goods yard 'B4', and No 31556 at Brighton. The association of the 'Ps' with Brighton had been a long one.

In 1938 a new source of employment for these tanks arose following the aforementioned improvements undertaken at Kingston Wharf. Nos 1323 and 1557 were transferred to Brighton, one being employed as shed coal stage pilot and the other working at Kingston. Problems with buffer interlocking had led to a ban on the use of the 'Terriers' on the wharf, which on the face of it might have been the preferred choice, but the 'Ps' were to prove ideal for the job. Thus began a period of regular work that was to last until 1959 and the arrival of diesel power. Due to unavailability, other locomotives did substitute for the 'Ps' on occasion, including PD&SWJR 0-6-0T *A. S. Harris*,

Class 04 diesel shunter No D2296 is seen on the wharf in late 1961 alongside various items of debris – excluding the car, of course! The sharp curve, without (it may be noted) any check rail, is again proof of the need for short-wheelbase motive power. (The diesel had a wheelbase of just 9 feet compared with that of a 'P', which was 11 feet. By comparison that of a 'Terrier' was 12 feet and a 'B4' just 7 feet, which makes it all the more surprising that the 'B4' had previously been deemed unsuitable. The 'B4' type was well used to working around very sharp curves elsewhere, including Southampton Docks, Hamworthy and Winchester City. Might it even have been a simple case of familiarity compared with resentment against the interloper?) *Ian Nolan*

which was given a trial in 1938, Southampton Docks Co 0-4-0ST No 3458, and 'B4s' Nos 30091/92, but none could match the Wainwright engines in terms of suitability.

Dieselisation arrived in the shape of Drewry/RSH 204hp unit No 11222, which reached Brighton in May 1957 for training purposes. By the end of June it was in regular use at Kingston on the shunting duty (No 778), being stabled overnight in the transit shed at Shoreham, returning only fortnightly to Brighton for servicing. No 31556 took over for a couple of days in August when the diesel went to Brighton for adjustment, the 'P' continuing to deputise when required both at Kingston and at Littlehampton quay, when its usual 'Terrier' was unavailable. When No 11222 was subsequently sent to Eastleigh, No 31325 was despatched to fill the breach and 'Ps' were kept in business until March 1959 when Drewry No D2082, later designated Class 03, arrived after repairs to damage that had been sustained en route from Hither Green to Brighton. During 1960 No 31556 continued to hold the fort at Brighton, deputising on the works shunting duty for 'A1X' No 32635, formerly 377S, which became derailed in Brighton shed. It also still put in the occasional appearance at Kingston, being noted there on 26 January; sister No 31323 was seen on 6 February.

With their work drying to a trickle following dieselisation, there was no 'Hayling Bridge' factor to ensure the longevity of the 'Ps', as was the case with their 'Terrier' cousins, which were to last until the end of 1963. Had they proved suitable for the Hayling line, the 'Ps' might also have gone on for another three years, but tests in 1957 with No 31325 on the Hayling branch revealed that the small boiler of the class was inadequate for the purpose and the monopoly of the 'Terriers' went unchallenged.

No 31323 paid a final visit to Brighton shed on 26 June 1960 before being sold out of service to the Bluebell Railway. No 31027 followed in its tracks in March 1961, leaving No 31556 as the last representative of the class when, in the summer of 1961, painted black and with no visible signs of its BR identity, it too was sold, this time to James Hodson & Sons, flour millers of Robertsbridge, becoming that company's *Pride of Sussex*. It was later sold on to the nearby K&ESR. The Bluebell acquired a third representative, as a source of spares, when Bowaters & Lloyds, which had bought No 31178 out of BR service in 1958, sold it to them in 1969. It then passed to the Port Line Project in 1989, which subsequently restored it for use on the Bluebell line.

So it is a remarkable statistic that today 50% of a relatively insignificant class of tank engine has ended up in preservation, which must surely be something of a record. They were found to be ideal locomotives for the early services provided by nascent preservation lines, and perhaps in this had found their true niche.

Freight services continued at Kingston Wharf until 1968, and in 1972 BR sold the wharf to the Shoreham Port Authority. Currently the 3.96 acres of the wharf are being advertised to developers as a major 'Waterside Residential/Mixed Use or Commercial Development Opportunity'. A far cry indeed from the days of the Dieppe packet!

Rebuilt

The letters and comments pages

The saga of red coaches rolls on…! This is 'M7' No 30027 at Bentley with the 12.50pm branch train to Bordon on 19 April 1957. *Norman Simmonds*

For whatever reason, recent issues appear to have generated rather more than usual in the way of comments, and with one exception, that from Alastair Wilson, this does not include No 44 – any comments from that issue will appear later.

We start with retired Loco Inspector Mark Abbott – and the **'Millbrook' image** in **'SW43'**:

'Dear Kevin, The train was not at Millbrook but to the west of Totton just before the Fawley branch off to the south. The Fawley line started from Totton goods yard and was not at Millbrook. The signal behind No 30117 was the Totton up distant.

No 30117 is on a horse box/cattle truck special to Beaulieu Road for one of the annual pony sales held mainly in October. The railway vans were used before horse boxes came into regular use, the horse boxes being used for riding ponies and the cattle trucks for less grand animals. They were sent to many destinations by rail.' [So two classes of pony travel as well! – Ed]

Regular reader Roger Macdonald also commented in similar fashion on the location as well as correcting a 'slip of the digit' for the caption on **page 36**: the 'M7' illustrated should of course have been stated as No 30105. As Roger puts it, '…another Bournemouth stalwart withdrawn in June 1963.'

Now to John Newton and 'Any colour as long as it's red' (**'Rolling Stock Files'** in **'SW43')**.

'I was interested in the piece in "SW43" concerning the "red" used on Southern Region suburban stock in Terry Coles's rolling stock files No 40.

I used to travel on the Exmouth branch daily during the '60s and my memory is of stock whose colour seemed much closer to the birdcage set No 520 on page 53 than that of push-pull No 650 on the previous page. Equally, the pictures of the "Compass Rose" tour in "Rebuilt" seem far too garish. Perhaps they had just had a repaint for the day – unlikely but not impossible, I suppose. Perhaps here a comment made in an Exeter model shop of that period is worth recalling. A (friendly) argument about the correct livery for a Western Region locomotive was brought to an abrupt halt when a retired WR driver commented, "They were never the right colour until they had travelled the seawall to Newton Abbot a few times"! Admittedly the Exmouth branch didn't experience the same force of the sea that we know can affect Dawlish, but the Exe is tidal and must have left its mark.

The piece on Health & Safety (**'Rebuilt', page 61**) also brought back a few memories of the time some friends and I wanted to reach the river beyond the track near Lympstone. We could not, of course, be asked to find a stream underbridge to do so, so instead, being very conversant with the timetable, we knew we were perfectly safe crossing the tracks. A wire fence guarded the line, which we duly scaled. On the inside of the fence I was surprised to find a wire that gave way too much when I stood on it, but a quick glance down the line showed a distant signal going up and down in unison with the pressure I exerted.

Also there was a permissive footpath between Lympstone and Exmouth, which for a mile or so ran beside the ballast inside the fencing. We had been happily cycling along it when we reached a stile back to a path outside the fence again. Dismounting and glancing back down the track I was rather disconcerted to see a Class 3 '82xxx' tank with the usual five coaches only about 100 yards behind us travelling at some speed. We hadn't heard it and presumably the crew hadn't seen us as they had sounded no warning! Ah, Health & Safety, what escapades you have spoiled...!

Now a most interesting, albeit brief, post from Nicholas T. Smith in Chippenham. This concerns **'45671 and our enquiry as to LSWR class designations'** from **'SW43'**. Nicholas writes:

'45671 was the pen name of A. John Powell. As for the "15" in D15, H15, N15, S15, it is just a sequential number as part of a cyclic series of works orders that work through the alphabet with a numerical suffix. Adams used it at Stratford (where it survived until 1923, and tenders had their own classes), and took it with him to the LSWR where it also survived until 1923. Bought-in classes used the loco numbers.'

From Alastair Wilson, with reference to **'Portsmouth Direct'** and **'Selsey Tram'** in **'SW44'**. (Alastair has been involved from an early stage with 'SW' and we remain ever grateful for his guidance and foresight.)

'As always, it's a pleasure for me to see each issue of "SW" when it's still in its "birthday suit", as you might say, and to try and visualise each image from its caption only. There are a couple of comments to be made about "SW44" that I hope may interest other readers.

In his piece on the "Portsmouth not-so-direct line", Jeremy Clarke remarked that the junction station at Bishopstoke became Eastleigh from July 1923. I can say with certainty that it was referred to as 'East Leigh' or 'Eastleigh' long before – in 1901, to be precise. One of my other interests is the author Rudyard Kipling, and I have recently been transcribing for the members of the Kipling Society what remains of his wife's diaries, now the only first-hand account of his life on a day-by-day basis.

On one day in December 1901, Carrie Kipling recorded, "We make an early start, travelling by saloon to Southampton. Pater meets at Eastleigh. Start on SS *Kinfauns* at 5 pm."

The Kiplings were then living at Rottingdean, and were about to embark for their annual winter visit to South Africa (Kipling had been told he should avoid English winters after a near-death bout of pneumonia in 1899). They'd made the trip a year earlier, when they'd taken normal trains. They had two children and two nursemaids, and a mountain of baggage (heavy steamer trunks "not wanted on voyage" and a mass of other luggage), and the porters at stations where they changed trains must have blanched at the task of identifying it all and transferring it from one luggage van to another. So this year they "went a bust" and hired a private saloon from the LBSCR to take them from Brighton to Southampton (Kipling was a very rich man, then at the height of his earning power as a writer. In 1895, for example, he earned £354 for one short story, which took him a month to write – it may not sound very much, but at 2018 values that's about £32,000. As I say, he was a very rich man and could afford to have a private saloon.)

There's no indication of whether they travelled via London or along the coast, but my guess is that they went Brighton-Fratton (LBSCR), Fratton-Bishopstoke (Eastleigh) (LSWR), and Bishopstoke (Eastleigh)-Southampton Docks (LSWR). They were joined at Eastleigh by Kipling's father who was accompanying them to South Africa. He lived at Tisbury, and had presumably taken a local to Salisbury, thence via Romsey and Chandlers Ford to Eastleigh, where he joined the Kipling's saloon for the last 15 miles or so to the docks, where they would arrive in state! Again, I would love to know for

On Tuesday 10 July at Tonbridge station booking hall there was an unveiling of a blue plaque to commemorate Colonel Stephens – in the opinion of many, long overdue. The actual unveiling was carried out by Les Darbyshire, who is seen in the individual view and also third from the left in the group image. The others present are (l to r) Pat Walsh, Station Manager, Tonbridge; David Wornham; and Ian Legg, Chairman of the Kent & East Sussex Railway. With grateful thanks to Ross Shimmon.

certain, but I think it probable that their saloon was worked forward as a "special", rather than being attached to a boat train at Eastleigh.

My other comment – well, comments – relates to the piece on the "Selsey Tram". First of all, does anyone know what the author of the report, E. S. Cox, got his MVO for? Membership of the Royal Victorian Order is in the personal gift of the Sovereign (it's not a Government-sponsored honour), and is usually given for some form of service to the Royal Family – for example, it might include making the arrangements for a major Royal railway journey.

I lived, until a couple of years ago, for 55 years on the northern fringe of the "Hundred of Manhood" and came to know the whole area between Chichester and Selsey pretty well and walked various bits of the Tramway's route (such as are now accessible). A "Hundred" was a medieval land area, and there still is a Manhood End Farm on the A286 about 2 miles SW of Chichester. My comments follow the sequence of Cox's report.

History and Legal Status

Cox talks about the "Registrar at Somerset House". In those days, Somerset House, just off the Strand in London, was the place where company records were kept – today, there is a Companies House in Cardiff, to where all records and returns go.

Topography

Messrs Sadlers was an important Chichester firm of agricultural merchants, and members of the Sadler family were part of the "mercantile aristocracy" of Chichester, together with the Covers, Purchases and others. The firm is no longer trading, since the 1990s, but the name lives on in various developments inside Chichester city.

The "occupation road leading to Messrs Sadlers" is now Terminus Road, about a mile long and the site of one of Chichester's major industrial estates.

Regarding the Stockbridge Road crossing, there was then no east-west bypass, and the Stockbridge Road, the A286, is the main road into the Selsey peninsula (north-south at this point), leading to East and West Wittering. The tramway crossed it about three-quarters of a mile south of Chichester station, running NNW-SSE, close to the junction of the B2145, the Selsey Road, and the site of a pub named "The Selsey Tram", (demolished in the last five years or so). The whole area is now covered with housing, but in 1923 Stockbridge was no more than a hamlet.

Regarding the Canal Drawbridge, the canal is running more or less north-south and it was on this stretch that the painter J. M. W. Turner painted Chichester Canal in 1828 – the canal looks much broader then than it is today, and Turner painted a sea-going ship in it. But just before reaching the village of Hunston, the canal makes a right-angled turn to run just south of west towards its exit into Chichester Harbour at Birdham, and the tramway had to cross the waterway by means of a drawbridge, so that canal traffic could pass – there was still infrequent commercial traffic up to Chichester when the line was constructed. In fact, the Chichester Canal was an arm of the Portsmouth & Arundel Canal, completed in 1823, which ran from the River Arun at Ford to Chichester harbour; the section from Ford to Hunston, meant for nothing bigger than a barge, had been abandoned in 1855. It is now largely de-watered, but it can still be traced for much of its course. However, the dog-leg Chichester-Hunston-Birdham section was built as a (small) ship canal and is maintained for pleasure traffic.

Cox's comment about the County Council having replaced the A286 road bridge with culverts remains true today, and is a major reason why various plans to restore the canal for its whole length for leisure traffic have failed. However, leisure boat traffic occurs on both sides of the road crossing.

Hunston

The village has expanded and now extends further along the Chichester-Selsey road, so that the site of the station is now in the middle of the village, although no trace of it remains. After Hunston, the line heads off into the country.

Chalder Station

Sidlesham is still in two parts, and although there has been some development, it has not yet suffered having a large new estate annexed to it, possibly because the roads to Chichester, which sufficed for enough traffic to kill off the tramway, are totally inadequate for today's traffic.

Sidlesham

There's a reference at the end of this sub-section to the line "being carried on an embankment constructed after the sea break in 1910". Up to the 1870s there was a large inlet on the east side of the Selsey peninsula, known as Pagham Harbour. In 1873 the narrow mouth giving on to the sea was blocked, and an attempt made to drain the saltmarsh lying behind. When the line was built in 1897, the whole of the Selsey peninsula was low-lying farmland, much of it just below sea level. In a massive storm in December 1910 Mother Nature took charge, and washed away the newly created (30-odd years) shingle bank across the mouth of the inlet, re-flooding the former saltmarsh. Half-hearted attempts were made to restore the closure of the inlet, but they were ineffective and the area was allowed to return to what it did best – being a natural inlet. It is now a major nature reserve, especially for seabirds.

Ferry

There was no ferry, but there had been one in times past to take travellers to Selsey over the inner end of Pagham Harbour.

Selsey Bridge

The ground here is largely shingle, and the "ballast pit" provided the shingle ballast on which the line was laid.

Ways and Works

Mr W. H. Austen was Colonel Stephens's right-hand man and successor. He ran the empire from the office in Tonbridge and his name appeared at the foot of virtually every bit of paper that related to the management of the railways of the Stephens empire.

Wagons

As will appear later, the railcars ran back-to-back with the "special truck" sandwiched between then for passengers' luggage and parcels.

Territory

The population figures are interesting. Growth was slow in the years between the wars – the great expansion came in the post-war years, and was then largely bungalows for retired people, to the extent that the area to the east of the tramway, round the hamlets of Pagham and Rose Green, became known locally as the "Costa Geriatrica".

One development that Cox does not mention (it would not then have much affected the tramway) was that in the immediate aftermath of the war a substantial area of the land, which was 'pastoral in character, though beet sugar is grown' and lay east of the railway, between Hunston and Pagham, and another large parcel that lay between the A286 (the main road to the Witterings) and the Selsey road, south and west of the railway, had been acquired by the Land Settlement Association, and was to be used to settle soldiers returned from the war who wished to establish themselves as market gardeners. Between the wars, these gradually flourished, and a thriving trade in cut flowers and tomatoes in particular grew up. Today, there are very large areas of glasshouses in the area, and many of the smaller nurseries have sold out to a big Dutch combine. In the 1920s only a small portion of this trade might have come to the railway – the distances to the railway were mostly 2 or 3 miles, so a small truck would have been necessary, and it would have been as easy to take traffic for London, and Covent Garden, straight to Chichester, so avoiding the need for transhipment and possible damage to blooms and fruit.

The one holiday camp has now grown into several, and a number of trailer parks. The "lobster fishery" is still substantial, and "Selsey crab" is popular locally.

Chichester's population is now 27,000, but that is, literally, the city and does not include the population of its "suburbs". The total population is now well up to the 50,000 mark.

Messrs Shippams continued to make its fish paste and other delicacies at a factory inside the main shopping area until it was taken over and moved to a new factory in the Terminus Road industrial estate in 2002.

The sugar beet factory never appeared, though substantial quantities of sugar beet continued to be grown in the area, and was transported by rail to East Anglia for processing until the late 1960s, using the closed station at Lavant, then the northern end of the truncated Chichester-Midhurst branch, as the loading railhead.

Traffic and Revenue

(b) Passengers

The drop of 22.25% in passenger numbers in 1920 was largely due to increased competition from motor buses as young men returned from the war, having learned to drive, and invested their gratuity in a bus, or even two. They competed with the established bus company, Southdown, until the latter bought them out.

Present Position

Sub-para (b)

Chichester had bay platforms at the west end on both the up and down sides. They were used mostly for the "motor trains", which provided the stopping services to Portsmouth. When electrification came, the services were provided mostly by a single 2-NOL unit, while later 2-BILs were the usual stock.

Conclusion

In our introductory paragraphs, mention is made of a tentative proposal that the Selsey line, had it been acquired by the Southern, might have been electrified. Well, yes, but not immediately; the main line through Chichester, with the branches to Bognor and Littlehampton, was not electrified until 1938, and I would suggest that the Selsey line was more likely to have been treated like the Hayling Island branch and left to steam.

Also of interest, and not mentioned by Cox, was the suggestion – proposal is too definite a word – that the Selsey railway might throw off branches, eastward to Pagham and south-westward to the Witterings, with Hunston becoming a mini-Clapham Junction, Now, there is a thought! Such things would have been wildly uneconomic in the 1930s up to the 1990s, but the road network in the Selsey peninsula is now hopelessly inadequate as more and more houses are built in the Manhood, without adequate infrastructure. Whether one tries to get to Chichester for work or shopping or to the hospital, or to access the A27 trunk road to go east or west, traffic jams are the order of the day, and in the rush hours a 12-minute trip from Birdham to Chichester can take 40 minutes, as a matter of course. This makes trying to use Chichester as a commuting railhead an impossibility. Meanwhile, on summer weekends the A286 is chock-a-block with cars flowing in in the morning and out in the evening. So the lack of Class 377s, humming their way to Selsey, becomes a matter of some regret.'

Now from John Raggett on the topic of **Tony Molyneaux's colour feature**, in particular page 37 of **'SW43'**.

'As always, an excellent issue, especially the superb colour photos of Tony Molyneaux. May I add some comments relating to the steam-hauled EMU move? Not wishing to challenge Mr Marsden's expertise, I suggest that this is merely a stock move, presumably to Wimbledon Park. In 1960 the SR built the first of two batches of 4-EPBs to BR standard design, numbered 5301 to 5356. However, the first two had Bulleid SR trailers and I suspect the unit next to the loco is either No 5301 or 5302. Looking under the magnifying glass, you can indeed see the BR roundel on the sides of cars four and six. You can also just make out the white, opaque toilet window part way along the side of car five, making the trailing unit a BR standard 2-HAP – unit No 6161?

Another from the Tony Molyneaux archive, showing No 31803 on the down main just south of Swaythling station on 24 March 1961.

Southern EMUs went to Eastleigh for overhaul, etc, and until electrification in 1967 had to be hauled by loco, running as unbraked "freight" trains with a brake van. Often this would be via Fratton or Chichester, from whence the units could make their way under their own power. After electrification stock from all across the SR would often circulate via Wimbledon Park and run to and from Eastleigh under its own power, for which there was a scheduled daily pathway in the WTT. I remember seeing such a working with a 2-BIL rattling down the fast line at Woking in 1967 with headcode 91. That said, I also remember seeing a Class 33 detaching freshly painted EMUs in the electrified reception road at Chichester around 1970, so not all EMU moves went via the SWD under their own power.' [See also the comment by Greg Beecroft later in this section – Ed]

Now from Jim Gosden on **'The Lost Archives of Stephen Townroe'** in **'SW43'**.

'What a treasure trove we have in the lost archives of Stephen Townroe. With his ability to have access to locations and areas of the Southern Railway that the amateur enthusiast did not, and with an engineer's interest and eye, he took photographs of quite ordinary objects and scenes that have ceased to exist with the passage of time. These have now become precious in recording the details of railway history.

'With regard to SCT's photograph on page 54 of "SW43", looking along the side of a "Merchant Navy", I am 100% certain that I know the location of the cutting. It is even further east of Byfleet than your guess.

I was born and bred at Hersham near both Walton-on-Thames and Weybridge and knew the area intimately as a youth. I believe the location is Oatlands cutting and that the train is on the down main line heading west. There appears to be a milepost on the left – all the mileposts were on the down side. This one I suspect is the 17¾ milepost (from Waterloo).

Oatlands cutting is over a mile and three-quarters long and lies between Sir Richard's bridge, which is about a quarter of a mile from Walton station, and Haines bridge in Weybridge; in fact, it extends beyond that bridge right up to Weybridge station, which is 2 miles from Walton station at 19¼ miles from Waterloo. I think the train is about halfway along the cutting, probably just past Oatlands signal box, and through the haze can just be seen Haines bridge over the line. You mention that the image is one of four, so it is possible that one of the others is nearer to Haines bridge and clearer in outline.

Oatlands cutting is certainly one of the longest, if not *the* longest, on the old LSWR main line out of Waterloo. It probably ranks with Sonning cutting on the GWR, but is not as well known as there are no intermediate access points along it.

In 'SW' No 5, page 76, you published a photograph of mine showing Southern diesel loco No 10201 in Oatlands cutting on a down express at about the halfway point and looking towards Walton and the aforementioned Sir Richard's bridge, which can just be seen.

Further to my email of yesterday, I have referred to an old 1-inch OS map of the area and now believe the milepost I thought to be 17¾ is in fact the 17½ from Waterloo.

The whole length of the cutting is also a mile and three-quarters from Sir Richard's bridge to Weybridge station, which is some length!'

Now from 'Graham 1952' with reference to **'Imperial Airways and the Southern Railway'**, which appeared in **'SW43'** – not all railway, but I think that, like me, many will have a wry chuckle over Graham's comments.

'SCT' took four views on the trip referred to (his reference 'Album 9 Negs 1-1 to 1-4'). We may reasonably assume that they were all taken on the same day and on the same train. In 'SW43' we used Neg '1-4'. This one is Neg '1-2', and with the train therefore on the up line we may again conclude it was taken earlier on the journey. With a line clearly coming in from the left, the initial belief was that this was either Pirbright Junction or Sturt Junction, but with a station in the background...? 'SW' readers are excellent at identifying locations, so some help on this one would be appreciated! (The others, Negs '1-1' and '1-3' are of no assistance.)

A repeat from a few years ago of Jim's image of the cutting, which appeared in 'SW5'.

He starts with a comment regarding some difficulty in obtaining his copy (remarks we have passed on to the office), but then continues:

'Well, it was certainly worth the wait! You have set a very high bench-mark so I'm always eagerly anticipating the following issue. I recall my time editing *The Tennis Times*, another quarterly publication, and feeling the pressure to keep raising the quality of content. I have no doubt that you will continue to keep us all enthralled.

Thank you for raising the issue of loco category numbering; I raised it with the SREmG and received a number of replies – perhaps the most convincing suggested that S15, H15, etc, were never intended as loco class designators but were related to a Works Order numbering system. It certainly sparked healthy debate. I was also delighted to see the little teaser on loco naming – plaudits to Alastair Wilson and his info on the Stirling "F" Class loco.

I loved the piece on the redoubtable Col Stephens – what a different and less regulated world it was back then. As ever, Stephen Townroe's lost archives are fascinating – the photos of the shovel and the reference to eggs and bacon cooked on it took me back to Salfords station in the late 1950s and my morning on the "Q" Class shunting coal wagons in the Hall & Co yard – bacon never tasted as good again! As an ex-girlfriend came from Caterham, I was very pleased to read about the development of the service. In fact, I have read and re-read the issue from cover to cover and thoroughly enjoyed all of it.

Your piece on the Southern Railway and Imperial Airways (wish I could have afforded the Hornby train pack) struck a chord as both my maternal uncles worked for BOAC, as did I, and Bob visited Poole in Imperial Airways days. Indeed, BOAC was Poole's largest employer, having created nearly 650 jobs. He used to fly down to South Africa quite regularly as he was involved in airline and air service administration and regaled me as a child with some of the more interesting tales of the flying boats and their crews and passengers. Of all the many stories, though, it was something else that stopped me in my tracks – a fascinating note from January 1944 that read 'Pierrepoint and assistant to Gibraltar – top secret – not a good flyer'. It turned out that Albert Pierrepoint, Official Hangman, and his Assistant Hangman were flown secretly from Poole Harbour to Gibraltar to hang two young Spanish men who had been caught working for the Abwehr, the German Intelligence Service, on the island, one being a saboteur and the other more of an intelligence gatherer. Quite why it was necessary to fly out Pierrepoint under a cloud of secrecy to carry out the executions by hanging during time of war is a mystery to me. It was only in the summer of the previous year over the Bay of Biscay that Leslie Howard had been killed on BOAC Flight 777 when his plane was shot down by the Luftwaffe. Although Axis airpower was much less of a threat in January 1944, Pierrepoint's mission was not without risk.

We rightly bemoan the loss of a number of Southern loco types that never made it into preservation; the same can certainly be said of all of our British-made flying boats – as far as I'm aware, not one was saved. One of my favourite stories concerned one of the flying boats – it may have been a Short – which suffered a bird strike that damaged the leading strut on one of the wing floats and the pilot was forced to make a precarious landing on Lake Tanganyika or Victoria. The Purser/Chief Steward was obliged by the Captain to enquire of the three lady passengers if they had any nylon stockings – a delicate matter back then – and a very wealthy American socialite produced a supply. Whereupon the poor Purser was required to enter the water, swim to the float, clamber onto it and effect a temporary repair to the shattered strut by binding it with three pairs of nylon stockings, secured additionally with melted wax from a seal thrown to him by the crew. A nervous take-off ensued, but all was well and the lash-up survived the landing at

Continuing the theme of 'unknowns' and asking for readers' help, Roger Simmonds recently submitted this view. We are reasonably certain it is LSWR – judging by the look of what are railway cottages in the background – and what could well be a separate office for the Station Master, as was often provided in such fashion. But any ideas where? (The sign on the edge of the building was defaced on the original image.)

their intended destination, a proper repair then being undertaken. Thank goodness there weren't Health & Safety regulations in force back then. Just imagine: "OK, simply take the stockings, ignore the crocodiles and get to the float..."

Enough about aviation – I wonder if Nigel Tilly will get an answer to the mystery of 41295...?'

Further proof that we are primarily a railway publication, and stray away from our core area at our own risk, comes next from Steve Williams, again with reference to **'Imperial Airways'** in **'SW43'**.

'Dear Sir, I smiled when I read that Westland Wessex G-AAGW was supposed to have survived until 1964 ('SW43', page 6). This relic was lucky to have made it to the 1940s, never mind the 1960s! Its last Certificate of Airworthiness expired on 16 August 1940 and, as the Air Ministry declined to impress it for RAF service, it faded away into wartime oblivion.' [Steve, it is appreciated and we are delighted to put the record straight – Ed.]

Finally on the subject of **'Imperial Airways'** in **'SW43'**, this from Greg Beecroft:

'A most interesting article in "SW43" concerning the Southern Railway and Imperial Airways/BOAC. It would be interesting to know who was using the air service during the Second World War; presumably they would be senior politicians, government officials and the like. Ordinary civilians, even the necessarily wealthy ones, are unlikely to have been flying round the world then. There is reference to aircraft losses, not specified. Several flying boats crashed or were badly damaged by objects in the water. These included *Calpurnia*, which crashed when landing in Iraq on 27 November 1938, and *Cavalier*, which came down in the Atlantic on 21 January 1939. Quite the most extraordinary event concerned *Corsair*, while working from Durban to Southampton. Her direction-finding equipment became faulty and was replaced at Kisumu on Lake Victoria. The next stage of the journey, on 14 March 1939, was to take the aircraft to Port Bell, also on Lake Victoria, then to Juba, on the River Nile in Sudan. Unfortunately, the mechanics did not set up the direction-finding equipment correctly and the crew did not notice this while flying over the lake. Once over land, after leaving Port Bell, they were guided by the equipment and flew in quite the wrong direction. Hundreds of miles off course and with fuel running low, they managed to land the aircraft on the River Dungu in the Belgian Congo. The pilot was very skilful in getting the aircraft down, but it hit a rock in the river and was damaged. It had to be repaired and the river had to be dammed to create enough water space for *Corsair* to take off, which was achieved on 6 January 1940. An account of the Imperial Airways flying boat service, *Corairville: The Lost Domain of the Flying Boat* by Graham Coster, was published in 2000 (the paperback is ISBN 0 140 25348 3).' Greg also adds an unrelated comment on the **EMU image** on page 37 of the **Tony Molyneaux colour section** in **'SW43'**:

'I suggest that what this photograph shows is one of the four 4-EPB units that had BR-design motor coaches, but SR trailers. Presumably the rear two coaches are 2-HAP No 6161. The 4-EPB units concerned were Nos 5261, 5262, 5301 and 5302.' Next from Nicholas Owen on the piece on **'SR EMUs'** in **'SW43'**.

'Thank you so much for the splurge of Southern Electric pictures in "Southern Way 43". I hope I have never been one of those "certain detractors" you felt the need to appease. [This related to a note I made in response to receiving this note from Nicholas where I said I have been berated on occasions for sometimes including too much steam. No, Nicholas, this was never aimed at you – Ed] I am just delighted that the Southern gets such regular, well-informed, and interesting attention.

Still, it was so good to see electrics have such coverage. Many of the shots I haven't seen before. A few observations.

Look behind the 6-PUL leaving Victoria in 1937 and you will see the strange platform arrangement whereby three long approaching roads merged into two. Was this unique?

Marvellous to see the battery of tall semaphores on the approach to East Croydon. And the down "City Limited" was on the tracks that remind us that the fast roads were the easterly lot in those days.

Finally – on one occasion over a very agreeable lunch – I told the saintly (?) Editor of my fascination with EMU headcodes. I threatened him with a piece about them one day. I may still strike... [Please do – I am sure we will all look forward to it – Ed]

The 'Blue' era may be in full swing elsewhere, but as far as this 2-BIL set is concerned green still remains supreme – well mostly. Set No 2026 is seen entering Fratton in June 1969, reputedly forming a local Chichester to Portsmouth working. *Roger Holmes*

So, a couple of thoughts about the ones we see in this sequence. The PUL drawing into Lewes is showing "50". The caption suggests that this was changed to Victoria-Littlehampton runs. I am happy to be corrected. But in my time, going back to the early '60s, Ore-Eastbourne-Victoria workings carried "52". Littlehamptons were "16". Maybe there were further changes after the war?

Then the scene at the old London Bridge Low Level, which I knew so well, as it was the terminus for trains from my beloved Tattenham Corner branch. The caption talks of "chaos" after a fire at Cannon Street. Well, from the visible headcodes I suggest that "85" was for the usual Tattenham run; "82" was most probably a diverted HAL formation heading for Gillingham. If any other headcode aficionados are out there, please let's be in touch!' [I think this proves we *need* that article! – Ed]

Two views recently came into our possession concerning the guarding of signal boxes during the railway strike of July 1911. Both depict troops and police at what were considered 'key' locations, although there is no information as to whether this was simply a deterrent or in consequence of an actual or anticipated incident. We have been fortunate to have had access to the files relating to 'another railway company' relative to this period and from these it appears that certain locations, the London area especially, were considered to be more at risk of interference from strikers than elsewhere. The conclusion is that the same would have applied on most lines out of London regardless of company. Again, more information would be appreciated.

Next from a very good and, dare I run the risk of saying, old friend, Rob Thompson. Rob and I used to converse at any number of shows in the past, and while I am rarely at such events nowadays, it was good to catch up. I should also thank Rob for his support from the earliest days of 'SW', often with constructive criticism that I hope we have taken on board.

Rob's comments relate to several aspects of **'SW43'**, but we have decided to retain his letter in one place rather than attempt to split it and conjoin with other contributors. He starts:

'First time, I believe, I have ever written to you about an issue of "SW". What an excellent issue No 43 is, probably the first time I have read the whole magazine from cover to cover and within a few days of receiving it. The picture content is outstanding, particularly the Tony Molyneaux section. My hearty congratulations. However I have a number of comments and queries. In particular in the Holman Stephens article where a) on page 68 it is recorded that he "was apprenticed at the workshops of the Metropolitan Railway in 1881 as a pupil of..." By my reckoning Stephens would have been 12 or 13 at that time and therefore I assume it should read 1891, in which case b) in the next paragraph on page 68 it records his starting on the Hawkhurst project "at the relatively tender age of 22". If he was only apprenticed in 1891, then while it is just possible that he could have been on the Hawkhurst project at the age of 22, I feel it questionable seeing that he was born in 1868. As he would have been 22 on 31 October 1890 and only apprenticed in 1891, did he really start on the Hawkhurst project before 31 October 1891, when he would have been 23? Just possible, yes, but what happened to his apprenticeship? This is not a question relevant to the article, but to his age. Referring to the Tony Molyneaux photos, I have comments on both those on page 40. The top photo shows a very clean PMV/CCT in green "sometime in 1963". I would have thought that this date was very late for what looks like a just-repainted van in green, but I could be wrong. However, it is certainly interesting to see such a clean van at that date. With reference to the lower photo on page 40, I am pretty certain that the loco is not No 30763 *Sir Bors de Ganis*. Even with the naked eye it is possible to see that the last figure is a different shape from the first figure, the "3". I don't think the middle numbers look like 7 or 6 either. Now, having put the photo under a reasonable magnifying glass I believe the number is 30804, *Sir Cador of Cornwall*. With reference to your querying the date, No 30804 was not recorded as withdrawn until February 1962, so the date given would now be perfectly feasible. No 30804 was one of the last 12 "Arthurs" in service at the end of 1961 and based at Eastleigh, so this makes it much more likely that this is the loco in the picture. Note also the converted PMV in the siding, which is in maroon.

I also find the lower photo on page 38 interesting as it refers to the York-Bournemouth train. I think I have mentioned in the past to you that, having been at school in Loughborough and living just outside Nottingham, I travelled regularly on the reverse version of this train from 1953 to 1961 (actually Bournemouth-York from September to May, then Bournemouth-Newcastle from May to September). In all that time I never remember Mark 1 coaches being in the consist; one train was always ex-LNER coaches and the other was always a mixed Bulleid/Maunsell set, mostly Maunsell, and they ran in opposite directions each day. Therefore I would think that the photo represents the train after it was diverted from the GC. I'm not sure when this happened, but I believe it was diverted from Sheffield on to the LMR through Derby and Birmingham and on to the GW line there. In its GC-line days the loco changes were rigidly set with a change from SR loco to GW at Oxford, and from GW to LNE at Leicester. I only once remember a GW loco running through to Nottingham when the "B1" at Leicester failed, but there was one at Nottingham so the GW loco was removed there – there was always the fear of gauging problems with GW locos north of Leicester. The loco in this photo could have been changed anywhere, but most likely Derby, and it could be standing in as the date was the Thursday of the Whitsun Holiday week and there was maybe a shortage of locos being in the wrong place.

A final 'catch-up' image in 'Rebuilt', a drawing of the 'Pimlico Terminus' at Battersea of the West End & Crystal Palace Railway – later the LBSCR – before the extension of Grosvenor Bridge and on to Victoria. This station closed in 1860. (See 'SW42'.)

A 'field trip' to the Smithfield Triangle

Alan Postlethwaite

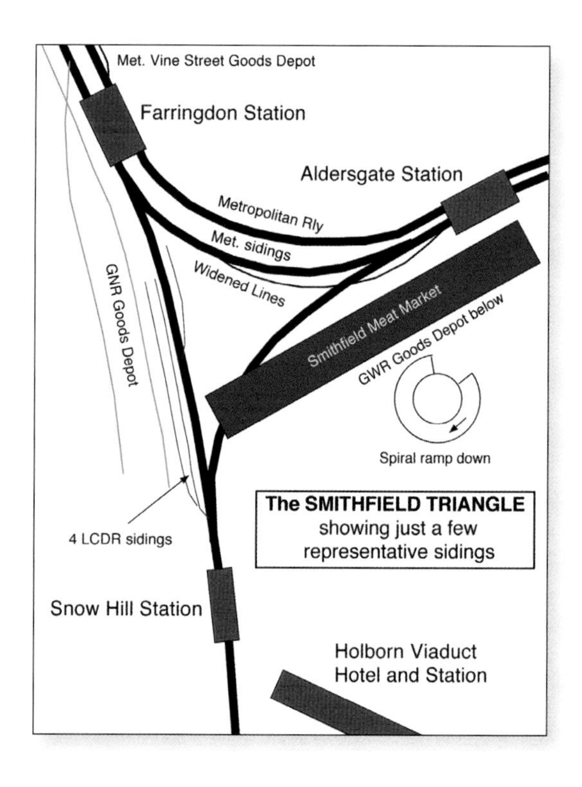

Passing the junction north of Snow Hill station is a Sunday Special from Hitchin to Brighton. Trains paused here for the banker to emerge from its siding near Farringdon. The line to the left leads to the LC&DR sidings. The curve to the right is bricked off, but was once used by LSWR push-pull trains on the Wimbledon-Moorgate service via Herne Hill. *John J. Smith, Bluebell Railway Archives, 1954*

During the late 1950s, Goldsmiths College ran extra-mural courses on Railway History as evening classes. One Sunday in March 1959, with the power switched off, there was a field trip to the City end of the LC&DR's Metropolitan Extension. Shepherded by an Inspector wearing the traditional long dark railway-issue coat, we walked from Blackfriars Bridge station to Blackfriars, Ludgate Hill and Holborn Viaduct stations, then to the Widened Lines at Farringdon. We entered the subterranean section down a wooden staircase from Snow Hill Road to the three-way junction just north of Snow Hill station. We continued into the unlit disused GWR sidings complex below Smithfield Market, where offices, loading bays and wagon turntables were numerous. Some of the turntables were intricate and unusual, including one with three tracks and another in the middle of a point. Two wagon hoists to ground level had been bombed at the beginning of the Second World War, stranding a few wagons on the upper level for years after.

We then continued on to the disused GNR goods depot by Farringdon station, noting its great warehouse and bollards for manoeuvring wagons by rope attached to either an engine or a horse. After this we returned via the LC&DR sidings to Snow Hill station, renamed Holborn Viaduct Low Level in 1912. Having passed Snow Hill signal box, buried deep in the tunnel, we then mounted the northbound platform where pillars and girders were being erected for a new building above. Five alcoves on this platform had once contained wooden seats for patients of St Bartholomew's Hospital to inhale the sulphurous exhaust fumes, considered beneficial to some at the time... We were also told that the walls of this station used to be whitewashed every week.

The climax of the visit came when a southbound goods train tackled the Snow Hill incline. The bellowing and hissing were heard in the distance, becoming a crescendo until, with a final burst of steam and smoke, a non-condensing tank engine appeared beyond a low brick wall. The engine panted furiously and the train slowed visibly as the main gradient was reached. Then the drumming of the diesel banker was heard, but it passed as an undefined mass since smoke and steam filled most of the air. To finish, we mounted a staircase to Holborn Viaduct terminus.

Used by some 11 Victorian railway companies, this underground extremity of the LC&DR held a wealth of railway history. The Metropolitan Railway carried east-west freight traffic together with the occasional Royal Train (Windsor-Sandringham), while trains queued patiently on Line 6 at London Bridge to use the north-south freight route to the GN and Midland railways. East Kent coal traffic for the Sheffield steel industry would also have used this connection to the GCR via Baker Street. We should perhaps spare a thought for those who spent their working lives in this gloomy, grimy, unhealthy labyrinth. It survives in sanitised form as Thameslink and the Metropolitan Line, freight and parcels having been transferred to rubber wheels on the M25. Records do not tell us how many patients survived the inhalation of sulphurous fumes; indeed, their ghosts may still haunt the line.

Inspired by this field trip, I have drafted a screenplay for a short film in glorious black & white. It stars Marty Feldman (or Jasper Carrott or Jacques Tati) whose simple task is to travel off-peak from Holborn Viaduct to Elephant & Castle. The booking clerk directs our hapless hero to the Low Level station for the next down train, where he promptly catches the 10.15 to Hitchin, 'down' being ambiguous here. Realising his mistake at Farringdon, he dashes to the opposite platform and jumps into the rear carriage of a train just departing. Sadly, it is the brake-van of a GWR goods train bound for Smithfield Market. The guard is not amused. Our hero is left to wander through the subterranean sidings to Aldersgate where he is advised to catch the next westbound train. Unfortunately, the next westbound train is Circle Line. In desperation, and by now thoroughly fed up with the railways, he decides to alight at Westminster to catch a tram. He knows for sure that all trams along the Embankment run via the Elephant. The first one happens to be a No 33, which takes him through the Kingsway Tunnel back to Holborn. And so on...

Demolition of buildings above Snow Hill station is seen in 1956. Alcoves can be seen on the northbound platform (left). The southbound platform (right) has offices and waiting rooms, as well as a catch point for the incline ahead. The signals are semaphore northbound and colour light southbound. Above and beyond is the fish building of Smithfield Market. *John J. Smith, Bluebell Railway Archives*

'D1' No 31741 climbs out of Snow Hill Tunnel on the wrong line, having collected empty goods wagons from the subterranean LC&DR sidings. *John J. Smith, Bluebell Railway Archives, 1958*

Looking east from Farringdon station road bridge, a DMU from Moorgate to Hitchin is on the Widened Lines. The Metropolitan/Circle lines and sidings are on the left. The LC&DR tunnel to Snow Hill is just to the right of this scene. *Alan Postlethwaite, Bluebell Railway Archives, 1962*

Charlie 'Knobby' Brown
Winchester shunter

We have spoken before about the importance of recording history from those who were actually involved, most importantly while that opportunity still presents itself. The railway could never have functioned without the men 'on the ground', be that the lowliest individual with a broom or the man (and it was always a man at that time) who directed operations from behind a desk. It may well be fascinating to read of the 'story behind the design' of our individual champions, Bulleid, Gresley, Churchward or Stanier, but again without the men who actually operated the products designed and provided by them there would have been no railway at all.

Such is the case of the railway shunter, a role and grade now extinct in its original form, for while a few locomotive-hauled trains still operate, albeit mainly freight, the number of times that coupling and uncoupling is required has been reduced to a minimum. Besides, I cannot imagine today's Health & Safety world permitting fly-shunting, or allowing a man to run alongside a moving wagon with a shunter's pole and brake stick (and add to this a hand lamp at night)! It was a skill now consigned to history, so it was with some excitement that I received a call from long-time friend Ian Shawyer with the words, 'I have found someone I think you should meet...'

That man was Charlie 'Knobby' Brown, to whom I was introduced together with his charming wife in the presence of Ian and his own wife Vera. (May I publicly say a special thank you to Vera for some excellent cake!)

'Knobby' had been the shunter at Winchester Chesil Bar End yard for a few short years starting in 1956/57 and ending around 1961/62. Now, before anyone starts complaining on

A shunter with his 'badge of office' – the shunting pole. Unfortunately it is not 'Knobby', but likely his replacement, photographed at Bar End in October 1964. By this time it was only goods from Eastleigh that were received or despatched, the line north of Winchester having been closed two months earlier. *Rod Hoyle*

the basis that 'Chesil had been a GWR location', I would counter by saying that it had been under the control of the Southern since 1950. To be fair, though, old habits and traditions die hard and, despite the fact that Knobby had joined BR(S), some of the older staff were still diehard Western men and to fit in Knobby had to join in their beliefs.

Sadly Knobby's memory is not all it once was, and some prompting aided by various photographs was needed. Once he got going, though, he was off, with tales of running after wagons, the various goings-on – some definitely *not* fit to print – and other odd snippets that he could recall but not the detail of the specific occasion or subsequent results. We are therefore left wondering about missing beer kegs, the behaviour of certain drivers, of railway lorry and steam engine, and perhaps most tantalising of all what did happen to those cattle that got loose one day?

When Knobby started there was a brief changeover period with the man he was replacing, after which he worked a five-day week on day shifts Monday to Friday. His first task was to deal with the up freight from Eastleigh, which only worked as far as Bar End before later returning whence it came. Goods loaded at Bar End destined for Southern lines would depart this way, as would wagons from north of Winchester that had arrived at the yard. As such Bar End was very much an interchange point and remarshalling point. A similar exchange took place for northbound traffic. Assuming that the traffic arriving was not 'full wagon loads' destined for elsewhere, the contents of each wagon needed to be sorted in the goods shed, then either repacked or consolidated in another wagon, or sent out for local despatch by one of the railway 'Scammells' based at the yard.

Knobby recalls that some of the Eastleigh drivers were not particularly polite to their junior firemen, although other men such as Alec Osman and Matt Sacree were the opposite. He recalls especially the tantalising smell of breakfast being cooked on the engine, something he has never forgotten.

After arrival, the Eastleigh men would shunt the yard as required, although naturally there would be some objections if the driver felt he was being taken advantage of. Once its train had been made up for the return journey, the Eastleigh freight would leave when it was ready, often ahead of the timetable, the passenger service being relatively infrequent. (Some readers may immediately cite this as proof that the initials GWR really did stand for 'Go When Ready'.)

Knobby admits that there was an awful lot of time spent drinking tea, often in cups with dubious hygiene, which took place in the 'new' shunter's cabin, the former engineman's cabin by the site of the engine shed that had closed some years earlier. During quiet times when all work was complete, Knobby could make himself comfortable and would on occasions be joined by the engine crews, the Eastleigh fireman charged with not only initially filling up the 'tortoise' stove but also ensuring that it was kept well stoked up. 'Good experience for you, lad...' was what the driver would tell his young fireman. But even the apparently simple act of having a cup or mug of tea might be fraught with risk, as witness the occasion when an enthusiastic young Eastleigh fireman thought he was doing his mate a favour by cleaning out the latter's regular tea-stained and encrusted mug. To say he was admonished is an understatement, the driver evidently being proud of the crust that had developed over the years in 'his' mug! Knobby's cabin even had a hammock strung across it and curtains at the window to keep out prying eyes! The building was also gas-lit.

Seen from the pedestrian footbridge that spanned the yard at the south end, an Eastleigh-based '80xxx' tank is engaged in its task. In the final days most traffic handled was coal, the majority of homes still using this as the fuel of choice. *Rod Hoyle*

Monday was usually the busiest day of the week, when both Knobby and the goods porter would be kept busy. On one occasion one of the two goods porters, a man who always carried a pocket watch, was asked if his timepiece was shockproof? When he replied 'Yes' Knobby borrowed it and pretended to place it under the wheel of the shunting engine.

After the departure of the Eastleigh train there was nothing much to do until the arrival of the WR goods from Newbury around mid-afternoon. Consequently this was the time he might wander up to the station to 'pass the time of day' and generally 'put the world to rights'. (Not a lot has changed in the 21st century!) Thus Knobby would come into contact with the men at the passenger station, the signalmen, booking clerk and porters. Long gaps between the train service could also lead to some interesting discussions. One of the passenger porters was a man called Albert White, who was also more than a little bit wary of the tunnel at the north end of the station. The porter's role included checking the tunnel if it was reported that a door was open when a train arrived at the station, which, according to Knobby, seemed to have occurred on a few occasions. As Albert was far from keen, apparently frightened as to what he might find, Knobby would take over. As he said, 'It was something to do.' The illumination available was of course no more than an oil handlamp, but nothing untoward was ever found.

Passenger services on the line were then shared between men from Eastleigh and Didcot, and Knobby recalls the story of one Didcot driver, who he could only recall as being known as 'Polly' and who had a stutter, who was suspended for two days without pay for overshooting the platform at Winchester.

Back at the yard the WR goods train would again be occupied in shunting until it departed late in the afternoon heading north towards Newbury. Knobby was not sure if the final destination was Reading or Didcot – it had certainly been the former in years past, then with the later departure time of 6.15pm.

Sitting back in his chair in Ian and Vera's conservatory that June morning, one could see Knobby's eyes filled with nostalgia as he spoke of times half a century and more ago. There was only one occasion when he recounted it had been not so good, and that was when, and for a reason he did not know, he was instructed to spend a week as relief shunter at the East yard at Eastleigh.

'That really was hard work,' he commented. 'I was on the go all the time ... busy place ... I was pleased when the week was over and I could get back to Winchester. I just wish I had kept my old shunter's pole as well...'

The lost archives of Stephen Townroe
Part 10

Preparing for departure at Waterloo, an unidentified 'Merchant Navy' backs on to its train ready for the 8.30am departure to Weymouth.

We have probably now reached about two-thirds of the archive, yet for the present still in Southern Railway days – just. Commencing this batch, we have a single train view, then straight into some of the topics we mentioned at the conclusion of the last selection.

Pages 76-79: **SCT took these views of lifting, blanketing then replacing the track at Walton, in the midst of which comes a single image of his motorcycle, a BSA, and the 'Bournemouth Belle' passing over a bridge at nearby Esher. The 45-ton steam crane from Guildford was being used, which may explain why SCT, as representative of the Motive Power Department, was present. There is no date, but by deduction it may be some time in the early part of 1947.**

WALTON-ON-THA

No reason is given for this photograph of main-line fireman F. 'Hampshire' Watts, although it was recounted by many that while SCT was to some a man to fear, he was also known for being fair and would stick up for his men if they were in the right. He also had an alleged habit of turning up unexpectedly – sometimes just where some might wish he had not been – regardless of the time of day – or night!

Opposite: This is likely posed image, but one with a definite leaning towards safety. Here, we are told, the fireman of a train on the up fast line, held at signals near Farnborough, is using the signal telephone to communicate with the signalman, while hidden from his view in his kneeling position another train approaches on the down fast line. With the noise from his own engine, it is unlikely that the man on the ground would have had much warning of the approaching train. Was this picture perhaps taken in consequence of an incident that had occurred?

Opposite page and above: **More p/way work, this time blanketing under the trackbed at Malden using concrete slabs. The date is May 1947, and the engineers have a 48-hour possession of the down local and down through lines. This time it is a p/way crane that is being used. Obviously there was also nothing worthy of entertainment in the area at the time!**

Right: **No, we have not gone 'all Western' (although there are around a dozen or so GWR images that we have deliberately omitted). Instead, this is included as this is Bowker's footbridge in the cutting just south of Shawford station, one end of which could be accessed from the end of the garden where SCT then lived. His family would at times stand on the bridge simply to watch the trains. The train being overtaken and hauled by No 5948 *Siddington Hall* is probably a stopping train from Southampton terminus destined for Reading.**

The final images in what is Album 9 are a loose strip of five negatives for which there is no record. Three are reproduced here, but in consequence of not having any information we can use only what the actual views show. (The two not used are of water gushing from an injector overflow.) First we have a loco inspector (?) alongside No 21C119 *Bideford*. Next we see some men clearly happy in their work, undertaking some task on a Bulleid coupling rod, and finally Nine Elms *before* those flats were built! No 21C12 *United States Lines* either coming on or going off shed.

We move now to the period June 1947 through to April 1948, starting with Geoffrey Chrimes. (T. E. Chrimes was the Motive Power Superintendent of the SR, so it is likely that Geoffrey was a relation, but we know not in what capacity he worked.) From the background it would seem that the view was taken at Nine Elms.

The penultimate item for this issue is a straightforward view looking east from Southampton Central. A 'T9' is approaching, while the parts of Southampton itself that are actually visible have changed out of all recognition today compared with 70 years ago.

Above and overleaf: **SCT was on the footplate of the first running trials of No 740 *Merlin* at the time of its conversion to burn oil. Tantalisingly we are not told where, but one suggestion is that it could well have been between Eastleigh and Salisbury. SCT deliberately makes note of the colour of the engine exhaust, and visibly it seems certainly no worse than an engine burning coal – but might that have had something to do with the fact that he was on the footplate? We also have a relative close-up of the oil pressure gauge on the footplate. Under the pseudonym 'Shed Superintendent', SCT also penned the following notes for the *Meccano Magazine* in September 1947:**

> **'The conversion of a number of locomotives to oil firing, as announced by British Railways last year, is not of course a difficult undertaking as far as the locomotives themselves are concerned, for this system of firing was in the experimental stage 50 years ago and has since been perfected. Fairly extensive ground installations at the Locomotive Depot must, however, be completed before the locomotives can be brought into regular service. Fuel oil is a dark, treacly substance that will flow readily when warm. This means that the storage tanks and pipe lines must be heated and the fuel tanks on the tenders of the engines as well. At each Depot installation a stationary boiler is required, not only to heat the tanks but also to provide a supply of steam to each engine that requires to be lighted up from cold.**
>
> **On an oil-fired engine, the burner, fixed at the front of the firebox under the brick arch, takes the form of a tray over which passes a jet of steam. Fuel oil is allowed to trickle on to the tray and directly it does so it is whisked off by the steam jet, which then becomes an inflammable mixture of steam and oil mist. When ignited, this jet is a sheet of flame, roaring in the firebox like a giant blowlamp. The pressure of steam at the jet and the rate of flow of oil are controlled by valves on the fireman's side of the footplate, and in the illustration [see Issue 44, and also that seen accompanying this piece] the necessary fittings can be seen on the right-hand side. The oil control and damper control are both on pillars. Six small hand wheels adjust the steam supply to the burner, blower, tank warmer, etc.**
>
> **The normal firehole door is locked, as it will be understood from the foregoing remark that the flame jet is directed rearwards towards the firehole door and it is not safe to open it while the jet is alight. A small mica window is fitted to the door, through which the enginemen can observe the flame inside the firebox.**
>
> **Control of the burner is a matter of training, although once the burner has been correctly proportioned to the design of engine, proper combustion occurs pretty well throughout the range of oil adjustments and on the road little more is necessary than to vary the oil supply with the rate that the engine is working. This needs considerable skill because the fireman must anticipate his driver's actions all the time turning on "the gas" well in advance of steam requirements and shutting down directly the throttle, or regulator, is closed.**
>
> **The fireman must also take care to avoid excessive smoke, but if the burner is correctly set in the workshops, and the dampers properly adjusted, smoke is barely perceptible at full load and any slight smoke will disappear when the engine has warmed up to its task. The consumption of oil is 5-6 gallons to the mile under load, and sufficient fuel is carried for a 250-mile journey, with the standard equipment now in process of fitting to main-line engines. This consumption may appear heavy, but very little oil is used when idling whereas a coal-burning engine has a fire on the grate all the time. Other advantages include rapid refuelling and a complete absence of ashes in the smokebox or ashpan.'**

Next time in this feature:
A trip into Devon at Wadebridge and Exeter; preservation of 'Terrier' No 82, with the loco on show at Dorking; accidents at Chertsey and Farnborough; some of SCT's involvement in the 1948 interchange trials; and the scrap sidings at Eastleigh.

David Vaughan interviews former Tonbridge fireman Gordon Castle

Gordon Castle spent ten years of his working life working on the Southern Region at Tonbridge shed. I started by asking him how he became an SR employee and why he chose the railway as a job.

GC I lived opposite the railway station at Ashurst and from an early age I always used to go down to the station and watch the trains. I told my father, I think when I was about six years old, that one day I wanted to be an engine driver. Later on, I bought my first *ABC* locomotive spotters' book.

At this point Gordon produced a well-thumbed early edition of *ABC British Railway Locomotives* with quite a few numbers underlined as 'spotted'.

A glimpse along the Chatham Dockyard branch, looking towards the terminus.

GC When I was about 10 or 11 I used to cycle about 6 miles to Hildenborough. My Mum would pack me up some sandwiches and a bottle of squash and off I'd go. I would sit on the bridge for about five or six hours and watch the trains go by. It wouldn't sound very exciting to today's kids but it's what we did and we enjoyed it. Where I went was of course the main line from Charing Cross through to Dover via Sevenoaks and there were all sorts going through, 'Schools', 'King Arthur', 'Battle of Britain' and 'West Country' classes as well as all the run-of-the mill goods and light passenger types. One of the things I remember well was seeing the Brighton 'Atlantic' that had been converted to try out various aspects of the experimental 'Leader' Class engine. These included fitting sleeve valve cylinders and a multiple blastpipe chimney. These modifications had turned a handsome looking engine into a bit of a monstrosity.

The line from Brighton to Uxted passed through Ashurst and was often used for locomotive testing, so I also saw 'Leader' itself come through. Other interesting engines I saw included the first two Fairburn tanks (forerunners of the Brighton-built Standard Class 4 tanks). They were Nos 42198 and 42199 and had 'BRITISH RAILWAYS' in large letters on the tank sides. I also spotted the experimental diesel No 10800, which had a single cab. I counted myself very lucky to be in the right place at just the right time and seeing locomotives that would not be seen elsewhere.

DV So when did you actually start working for the railway?

GC I was due to leave school at the beginning of the Easter term in 1955 but there were no vacancies at Tonbridge shed, which is where I wanted to go and work, so I ended up doing two more terms and left at Christmas 1955, starting work on 2 January 1956 at Tonbridge shed as a cleaner. As it was a 10-mile cycle ride to work in all weathers, it wasn't long before I got myself a little moped. There was a three-shift pattern: 6.00am-2.00pm, 2.00pm-10.00pm, and 10.00pm-6.00am. It took a team of four to thoroughly clean a 'Q1' and it was of course a very dirty job. Health & Safety was an unheard-of phrase and there were all sorts of hazards – open inspection pits, discarded fire irons and shovels, pools of oil and grease – and the lights in the roof were all smoke-blackened so visibility was pretty poor, especially at night when we had to rely on our oil lamps. Old baffle plates left lying on the ground were the worst, as they usually had a sharp and jagged edge to them.

DV When did you actually make the move from cleaner to fireman?

GC After about six months I was sent off to the firing school at Bricklayers Arms. We did a fortnight there, learning the various parts of the engine and the rules of the road. Then I went back to the shed and alternated between firing turns, mostly around the shed roads, and cleaning duties, so I suppose I actually started as a fireman in July 1956. I remember my first 'firing' duty was on an old 'E4'. It was used to supply air, created by the Westinghouse pump, to run the air tools in the fitters' shop, so I didn't actually go anywhere on it! I remember that the number of the engine was 32578.

My first real turn out on the main line was with a 'Q1' on a freight to Sevenoaks. By coincidence this locomotive was the first engine I had worked on as a cleaner. We always knew these engines as 'Charlies' because of the letter 'C' in the original Bullied numbering system. It wasn't the best of trips as it included the 2-mile-long tunnel outside Sevenoaks; this was always a wet tunnel and could give rise to slipping, which was not good under any circumstances, particularly so if you were in a tunnel.

DV I was told by another driver that the 'Q1s' were not very good riders as they were prone to rocking and rolling when going through points or over rough track.

GC Well, not so much rolling, more like jumping, especially on passenger trains. I had a mate on a passenger train to Ashford who was a bit heavy-handed on the regulator, and when he was on a 'Q1' he often used to shut off when going over points as he was afraid it would jump off the rails. Other than that, they were brilliant engines, reputed to be the most powerful inside-cylinder 0-6-0s in the world. We had ten of them allocated to Tonbridge shed because our duties included the heavy gypsum trains from Mountfield on the Hastings line.

DV Can you tell me about some of the more memorable turns you worked?

GC We had quite a few what we called gas-coal turns from Tonbridge to High Brooms gasworks. There were four round trips a day. They were 15-wagon trains, heavily loaded, the maximum load for a 'C' Class. There was a 1 in 47 to 1 in 53 gradient for about half a mile, so you got a run at it through the station; even so, by about halfway up the bank you were going so slow you could count the sleepers. There was one turn I remember, it was on a Monday morning when we were given 'C' Class No 31583, which had come off a passenger train from Maidstone. When I got on the footplate, the driver that we were taking over the engine from said, 'She's a bit soupy mate,' meaning that she had been priming quite a lot. Because of his words we took the engine on shed and cleaned the fire, the smokebox and the ashpan so as to start off in as good a condition as possible. At that time they used a special water-softening treatment in the form of chemical blocks put into the tender tank. These had the effect of taking all the scale off the boiler that had been building up for some time, but the disadvantage was that they also caused the boiler water to foam, so it was necessary to blow the boiler down regularly, which we duly did.

Anyway, my mate, who was Charlie Morphett, opened the regulator and straight away she primed. We set off with the steam cocks wide open as we would need all the steam we could get, so the safety valves were already blowing off as well. Unfortunately this meant that we were losing more steam than we were making. Anyway we set off up the bank but we could tell we were in trouble from the start and we had to stop about halfway and get a push from a 'Q1'. Owing to this incident Driver Morphett had to make out a 'Please explain' form, but it was only later that we found out the cause of the

Opposite: **An unidentified 'O1' is seen at Hawkesbury South Junction on 26 June 1953. One can almost hear the noise from the engine and the wheels and couplings straining on the sharp curve. To the crew it was all perfectly normal, something they had no doubt done numerous times in the past...** *W. A. Corkill*

poor performance of the 'C' Class. Apparently it had been working on ballast trains in the Gillingham area all over the weekend before working the passenger back from Maidstone. Water treatment chemicals had been used, but the locomotive had not been blown down once, despite the fact that it should have been done at the end of each duty; thus despite our best efforts with the aged boiler, priming was inevitable.

One of the coal train turns was at 1.45am in the morning, and when we had finished at High Brooms we had to shunt the yard at Tunbridge Wells Central goods. This took about 2 hours in the early hours of the morning. One thing about that particular goods yard was that it was an uphill shunt, meaning that we had to punch the wagons uphill, all this with a 60-year-old 'C' Class engine. Well, all this naturally created a good deal of noise but, although the yard was between houses in a built-up area, I don't recall getting any complaints from the residents. I suppose they were simply used to it.

Another turn I remember was a freight from The Wells to Battle, usually with a 'Q1'. We would run round the train at Battle, then go light engine to Etchingham and work the school train to Bexhill West. At Bexhill West there was a little loco facility, just a small shed really, where we could have a brew-up, and a small turntable that was a devil of a thing to work. It was hand-operated but more often than not you had to pinch-bar it round as it was so worn out. If you didn't get the balance just right the engine used to tilt over to one side, then you had no chance of getting it to go round. There were allotment gardens right up to the edge as well, and if we were not careful we would end up treading all over people's cabbages as we tried to push the thing round.

Another regular working for us was the gypsum trains from Mountfield. These were heavy trains, even for a 'Q1'. Mountfield was interesting because we had to go into a tunnel on a curve to get access to the siding. There was a bell that the guard pressed to let you know you had passed the 'dummy' signal at the other end of the tunnel, which we couldn't see, and that it was OK to enter the siding – you couldn't see it if you were in the tunnel of course. Another thing I remember about Mountfield was that there was a spring that came out of a bank in a pipe with lovely clear water; we used to go up there and fill our tea cans with it.

On another gypsum trip I remember it was a bit of a 'shucky' day and there had been a light shower of rain. Now a light shower is worse than a heavy one, as it is just enough to cause slipping on greasy rails, whereas heavy rain will wash the grease off. Anyway, we had just reached Stonegate when we started to slip and we just kept on slipping. It turned out that only one of our four sanders was working. We struggled on but just before Wadhurst Tunnel there were some curves, so not only were you fighting wet rails but also the friction of the rails. We slipped to a standstill and I had to get down on the line and sprinkle some sand by hand on the running line. We managed to get going again, which was just as well as there was one of the new Hastings DMU units not far behind.

DV It must have been around this time that the main London to Kent lines were electrified, wasn't it?

GC Yes, I remember that Sevenoaks Tunnel was closed at night as they were putting sheeting round the bore to prevent water getting on the third rail – this was another very wet tunnel. We were working the 11.05pm goods from Tonbridge to Bricklayers Arms with 'N1' Class No 31822. At that time all the class (of six) were based at Tonbridge, with No 31822 the worst one for steaming – I think the valve timing was out. Anyway, we were struggling all the way, and by the time we got to Godstone we were losing the battle to try and raise sufficient steam, so we stopped for a 'blow-up' for about 5 or 6 minutes. We had informed the signalman that we had stopped, of course. Now, it was a foggy night and a long train so we could not see the guard's van. Anyway we set sail for Redhill and when we got there, instead of going on through, they switched us into the siding that went down by the loco shed, which was a bit odd. The foreman came out and told us we had left the guard behind. He had apparently got out at Godstone to walk up and see what the trouble was, and he wasn't showing a light – at least, if he was we didn't see him in the fog. They stopped the night mail to pick him up and he eventually rejoined our train.

We eventually got to Bricklayers Arms but because we had been so long we almost had an empty tender. So we pulled on to the water crane and I jumped up on the tender to fill up. It wasn't until I was there on another occasion that I realised that while up on the tender I must have been very close to some live overhead electric cables. Now, the train was actually destined for Hither Green, but we had to go to 'the Arms' because of the tunnel closure. So we ran round the train and got on to the other end. The signal came off and we couldn't move at all, she just slipped to a standstill. The train had a 'fitted head' (vacuum-fitted stock marshalled next to the engine) and of course these vans were now on the rear end; the trouble was that the guard hadn't pulled the strings to release the vacuum brakes. Talk about a night to remember! Anyway, we did eventually get to Hither Green where normally we had about 2 hours before working light to Sevenoaks to work a passenger train back to Tonbridge. On this occasion though, and due to the delays, there was only just enough time to sort the engine out and grab a quick cup of tea before we were off again.

DV It just proves the old adage, 'What can go wrong will go wrong'! Anyway, please carry on. Where did you go from there?

'H2' 'Atlantic' No 32426 on an unknown working.

GC Well, we used to get situations where we were loaned out to other depots. I went to Redhill and to Stewarts Lane, but one of the more interesting jobs was to Folkestone Harbour. I did one shift of nine trips up the harbour branch to Folkestone Junction with the old 'R1' tank locomotives. It was all quite different from what I was used to: sometimes there were two engines at the front and one on the rear, or the other way round. On heavier trains there could be as many as three bankers. We could have got into trouble on one of the trips because I had a bit too much water in the boiler. As the engines entered the beginning of the 1 in 30 incline, just after the swing bridge, the water went to the back end so, with the safety valves blowing off ready for the climb, we had some priming. Of course, this was where there used to be cockle and whelk stalls with people milling about, and I am sure some of them got soaked with sooty water! It was all quite exciting, although there was not a lot of firing to do as the branch was only about three-quarters of a mile long, so when you got to the top you sorted out the fire and waited to go down either light or with the next down train.

DV I have fond memories of the Folkestone Harbour branch because an aunt and uncle used to have a house that overlooked it and I remember watching the 'R1s' pushing the 'Golden Arrow' coaches up the bank.

GC Another trip I did, which is memorable for all the wrong reasons, comes to mind. We used to do a trip to Ashford and go into the works from where we took over a goods to Galley Hill gasworks near St Leonards. On this occasion the engine was another 'C' Class, No 31112. It was supposed to be ready for us to go, but I looked into the firebox and there was this black fire with hardly any flame in it, and with only about 60lb of steam on the gauge. We didn't have long to get it ready, but we thought that, with the Romney Marsh line being pretty flat, we might get away with it – at least until we got to Ore, where there was a gradient. It ended up as a really awful trip and we struggled for steam all the way. It was at night, not helped by the fact that I didn't know the line very well, and with not many landmarks to go on I did not know where I was.

Anyway, as we approached the bank up to Ore we were on our last knockings of power. When you got to the top there was a tunnel, then the line dropped away at about 1 in 60 towards Hastings. My mate, Dave Batchelor, asked, 'Where do we usually stop to pin the brakes down?' I didn't really know but I told him I thought it was just outside the tunnel. Bearing in mind our lack of steam, he said, 'We had better not stop there.' We carried on but soon discovered that we could not stop going down the bank towards Hastings and we were a runaway. Obviously we screwed down the engine brake, shut the regulator and put the lever in reverse, but it didn't look as if it would slow us down enough to be able to stop at Hastings. I remembered that sometimes we went through the station, but at other times were switched into the yard. If we went into the yard at the speed we were doing we would have been in trouble because there was a set of catch points at one end of the yard and if we had gone through those we would have ended up in the road. As luck would have it we actually managed to stop at the end of the platform. We were relieved, in more ways than one, when the St Leonards crew took over for the rest of the trip, leaving us to work a gypsum train back to Tonbridge.

On the Brighton line we used to work the 10.30pm, the last Tonbridge working. It was a stock working, which meant that there were a number of empty coaches tacked on ready for the next day's services. We had a 'D1' 4-4-0, which was one of my favourite engines in many ways. We had five of those at Tonbridge when I was there (Nos 31487, 31489, 31492, 31470 and 31727.) No 31470 was my favourite as it had not long been outshopped from an overhaul and was in fine fettle. I had several memorable trips with a driver called Eddy Diplock. He would work the firehole door for you as you were shovelling to stop the cold air from going through on to the tubeplate. On one particular trip we were going into Lewes, and instead of going into one of the main platforms they switched us round the back, which meant you were on a curve so you had the weight of the train plus the friction of the curve against you as you started.

There was also a climb out of the station over the road bridge for the Cliffe High Street (the old Uckfield line, now closed). The inspector came up and asked if we wanted to set back so we could get a good start to counteract the adverse effect of the sharp curve and the gradient. Eddy said, 'No, we've got old 1470 – we'll be all right.' Anyway, we started off, then Eddy got his arm under the regulator and opened her right up and we marched out of the station in fine style. It must have raised a few echoes up the High Street, though!

An unusual duty that I remember involved a night out on the town, but not in the way that is usually meant. I was booked on with driver Bill Tomkinson at 7.50pm on a Saturday. First we went to London Bridge 'on the cushions', from where we walked to Bricklayers Arms depot and took over a 'D1' to New Cross Gate, where we picked up a train consisting of a mess coach, a steam crane, a bogie bolster carrying a large girder and a couple of brake vans. We went to Charing Cross station, ran round our train, then went on to Charing Cross Bridge while an engineering crew replaced one of the bridge girders. We stayed on the bridge over the Thames all night. My driver managed to fall asleep on the footplate but I stayed awake and watched the life of the river slowly return in the small hours. We did not return to New Cross Gate until 8.00pm on the Sunday and got to our home depot at about 9.30pm, by which time we had been on duty, although hanging around spare for a lot of the time, for around 26 hours, for which we were paid weekend overtime rates.

That just about brings me to the end of my steam days; I then went on to diesels.

DV That must have been quite a change for you. Can you tell me a bit about your diesel days?

GC Yes, well, I remember this one turn, it was on a freight, which must have had at least 50 wagons, from Tonbridge West yard to Hoo Junction. I was the second-man in the cab, which was normal for diesel crews in the early days. There is a steep bit before you get to Strood and you go through two tunnels, about 2 miles in length in total, and originally built for a canal. They are a narrow bore and cut straight out of the chalk; sometimes, with the exhaust blast from a steam engine, bits used to fall off. There was a gap between the two tunnels that was originally the passing place for the barges.

There is more skill in driving a freight than a passenger train, especially if it is loose-coupled. With a long train like that, as soon as the engine is over the summit you are still pulling, but when the rear of the train is clear of the summit the couplings all come back together, and as you regain speed you often feel the snatch as the couplings tighten again. Well there was a signal box as you came out of the second tunnel coming into Higham station and the signalman was holding out a red flag. On asking the reason he said, 'You've left the tail end behind, mate!' That meant of course that we had suffered a broken coupling. We were told to go into the yard at Hoo Junction and that the diesel shunter from Strood would push the tail end through. The upshot of that incident was another 'Please explain' for the driver, who was told that he should have read the General Appendix to the Rule Book, which stated that, in the event of a broken coupling, the crew should attempt to recover the broken part for subsequent examination. This would of course have involved us walking back through 2 miles of dark tunnels. I don't remember anyone ever actually doing that.

During the bad winter of 1962/63 we were on duty on Boxing Day when it first started to snow. It was a very cold and icy day and, although we did not know it at the time, the 'Night Ferry' from London to Dover had only got as far as Chelsfield. It was being hauled by one of the new 'E5xxx' electric locos, but due to excessive arcing at least one of the pick-up shoes had welded itself to the third rail. We were on an 'As ordered' turn

'H' Class No 31543 has just exited Mark Beech Tunnel on 23 April 1962, in charge of an Oxted to Tunbridge Wells West service.
S. C. Nash, Stephenson Locomotive Society

in the depot waiting for instructions when we were told, 'Go and rescue the "Night Ferry"!' This was a heavy train, usually consisting of ten sleeping cars and two baggage wagons, and in steam days was usually hauled by a 'West Country', often piloted by an 'L1' 4-4-0, hence we had to take two 'Crompton' diesels to do the job. When we got to the train they had 'paddled up' the shoes that were not affected and this freed up the electric engine, which we shunted into the yard at Chelsfield. We took the train as far as Tonbridge, where we were relieved, although by this time of course the train was running very late indeed.

Gordon left the railway in mid-1965 as he did not enjoy working on diesels as much as his steam days. However, he did not totally end his involvement with steam, as he worked as a volunteer fireman for the Bluebell Railway and, for a short period, on the Lavender Line. He also was involved as crew with various traction engines.

Book review: *Southern Style*
After Nationalisation 1948-1964

John Harvey HMRS

I first became aware of this book as a result of seeing it on James Hudson's book stand (a good man and well worth supporting) at 'Scaleforum' in September. I was impressed, although baulked slightly at the time at the £35 cover price for what is a 158-page paperback.

However, on this occasion first impressions were wrong and a later perusal indicated that here was a work written by a knowledgeable individual, well illustrated and similarly well produced.

My good friend Gerry Nichols has already commented on the work in the journal of the Stephenson Locomotive Society, and with his kind permission I quote from his review:

'While the Historical Model Railway Society (HMRS) has published livery information on various companies, primarily to enable those producing models to make accurate representations of the railway scene, the livery registers have always proved invaluable to those dating photographs or researching company histories. Having already produced seminal volumes on the London & South Western and London, Brighton & South Coast railways, the HMRS through John Harvey has produced this latest volume covering the Southern Region for the period from nationalisation in 1948 to the introduction of the Corporate liveries in 1964. While most of the book covers locomotives (steam, electric and diesel), the painting of passenger stock (both hauled and multiple unit) and almost everything managed by the Chief Civil Engineer is also addressed. The only exception noted by the author is that freight stock is not included, as the British Railways liveries were applied without variation.

The strength of this volume, which probably makes it unique, is that it is based on contemporaneous records from those involved and from those who decided in 1948 to record when each locomotive was renumbered and each major change of livery. The late Barry Fletcher was clearly the focus of this activity, but the roll call in the acknowledgements section is long and includes not only enthusiasts but also those within the railway workshops at Eastleigh, Brighton and Ashford. However, that is not to underestimate the role of John Harvey, who for at least 50 years has been researching Southern Railway liveries. Apparently the LMS-oriented design standards from the Railway Executive required adaptation and experimentation when applied to everything from a Beattie well tank to a Bulleid "Pacific", resulting in many variations. An interesting aside is that the Southern Region may have been able to make a financial case that "blood and custard" did not last as long as Southern green on the passenger stock and cost more than a single colour, resulting in the reversion to malachite green in 1956. To illustrate how comprehensive this work is, there is a full list of all locomotives that received the "S" prefix in the first quarter of 1948, together with the dates and styles of the painting of all Bulleid 'Pacifics'. Inevitably any such list cannot claim to be exhaustive, but the level of detail leaves little to be desired.'

With the opportunity provided by 'SW' I would also expand further on the formal content of '124 monochrome and 42 colour plates, 30 line drawings with separate card upon which are 13 colour swatches'. Many of these illustrations are new to me, both the colour and black & white, and they alone will appeal to some. Neither should this work be seen as one just for the modeller, as the historian and armchair enthusiast will find much to commend in recalling what was once commonplace. Indeed, how many of us would know exactly what was the exact hue under the all-pervading grime so reminiscent of the 1960s? The illustrations are well selected to complement specific points in the text, and while we probably all like to think we have a degree of knowledge of the subject at the start, I think is very likely that all will benefit from what can only be described as a scholarly work.

Six chapters, more accurately 'sections', describe Locomotives, Passenger stock liveries and Structure colours, both in general and then in specific detail. Assisting research is a comprehensive index.

In short – and I suspect that the reader will have gathered this already – this is an example of a book that should be on the shelves of every BR(S) enthusiast, and a few more besides.

ISBN 978 0 902835 35 1. Available direct from the HMRS or other good outlets.